SOUTH AFRICA

LANDMARKS

AND POPULAR PLACES

SOUTH AFRICA

LANDMARKS

AND POPULAR PLACES

PHOTOGRAPHS BY

AUGUST SYCHOLT

TEXT BY

PETER JOYCE &
BRIAN JOHNSON BARKER

STRUIK

Struik Publishers (Pty) Ltd
(a member of The Struik Publishing Group (Pty) Ltd)
Cornelis Struik House
80 McKenzie Street
Cape Town 8001

First published in 1991 by Central News Agency Ltd
This edition published in 1994 by Struik Publishers (Pty) Ltd

Reg. No. 54/00965/07

Editors: Valerie Streak and Jan Schaafsma
Designer: Odette Marais
Cover designer: Darren McLean

Page make-up by Suzanne Fortescue, Struik DTP
Reproduction by Unifoto (Pty) Ltd, Cape Town
Printing and binding by Tien Wah Press (Pte) Ltd, Singapore

ISBN 1-86825-650-2

C O N T E N T S

PREFACE

This book is something of a visual odyssey, a pictorial journey across the length and breadth of one of the world's most scenically varied, ethnically diverse and beautiful regions – a vast land of kaleidoscopic contrasts, vibrant, and steeped in tradition and history.

In a purely visual context the last-mentioned element – the historical – is most evident within the cultural heritage of South Africans of European descent, and a high percentage of the landmarks featured in these pages (the cities, their buildings and memorials) are the products of settler endeavour. The imbalance, if such it is, does not reflect subjective bias but, rather, the reality of the past. Bricks, mortar and monumental works – natural ingredients of a book such as this – are the legacy of urban civilizations; the indigenous, and mostly pastoral, peoples of southern Africa have other – no less enduring but less imposingly visible – legacies.

For obvious reasons our coverage has been selective rather than exhaustive, but the locations have been carefully chosen – for their visual quality, their popular repute, their intrinsic interest, and for their prominent place within the South African spectrum. We believe that they will appeal both to the traveller and the armchair browser, adding to their understanding of a country which, as this book goes to print, faces a challenging new era in its history.

AS, PJ, BJB

Knysna Lagoon's outlet to the Indian Ocean, flanked by the two impressive buttresses known as The Heads.

THE CAPE PENINSULA

TABLE MOUNTAIN

One of the best-known landmarks in the country, and indeed the world, Table Mountain towers majestically over the city of Cape Town and Table Bay in the northern segment of the Cape Peninsula.

The name given it by Antonio da Saldanha, the first white man to climb its heights (in 1503), is apt enough as it does indeed have a table-top summit, a prodigious one rising 1 086 m above the sea and stretching ruler-straight nearly 3 km from end to end. From the crest there are stunning panoramic views of the city and harbour, of the flanking Devil's Peak and Lion's Head buttresses, of Cape Point far to the south and of the blue-hazed Hottentots-Holland range to the east. On clear days, Table Mountain's massively distinctive bulk can be discerned fully 200 km out to sea.

ABOVE: *The broad sweep of Table Bay, its docks and, in the foreground, the handsome buildings of Cape Town's central business district – a bird's eye view from the heights of Table Mountain.*

PREVIOUS PAGE: *Table Mountain, distant but distinctive, viewed from Bloubergstrand – a seaside village north of Cape Town.*

Very often, though, the crest is hidden from view by clouds that billow across its rim and down its precipitous northern face to create what is known as the 'tablecloth'. This result of the strong south-easterly wind is an endless fascination to watchers in the streets far below.

Almost every one of the Peninsula's 2 600 plant species, collectively known as fynbos and part of the uniquely rich Cape Floral Kingdom, is found on the mountain's slopes and well-watered central plateau. Pride of place among them is taken by the shimmering silver tree (*Leucadendron*

argenteum) and the lovely wild red orchid *Disa uniflora* ('Pride of Table Mountain'). Hunters have long ago exterminated the bigger game, but the uplands and heights are now a protected area and a haven for baboon and antelope, civet cat, rock-rabbit, porcupine and a number of perhaps less welcome exotic species such as the Himalayan tahr, which resembles a cross between a sheep and a goat.

To get to the summit, one either takes the cable car or one of 350 charted paths, some of which are fairly undemanding and others exceptionally difficult. Climbers are urged to be cautious and to prepare carefully for the ascent as losing one's way can have disastrous consequences, especially if the massif's notoriously fickle weather suddenly takes a turn for the worse.

ABOVE. *The enchanted city. Cape Town's night-time sparkle is complemented by the floodlit grandeur of Table Mountain's northern face, rising sheer to a height of over 1 000m.*

HISTORIC
CAPE TOWN

The city is by far the oldest of the country's major urban centres. It was founded in 1652 by Commander Jan van Riebeeck and his small party of settlers as a replenishment station for the fleets of the Dutch East India Company's then great maritime empire. Today the metropolitan area fills the amphitheatre formed by Table Mountain, Lion's Head and Devil's Peak, then stretches southwards along both flanks of the Peninsula, northwards too, and also east across the low-lying plain known as the Cape Flats. Central Cape Town is, however, comparatively small. The main business district is little more than a dozen blocks square, and most of the historic sites are within leisurely ambling distance of each other.

RIGHT: *The Heerengracht, Cape Town's broadest and most elegant thoroughfare, links harbour and city. Its central island section supports lawns, palm trees, an ornamental fountain and some impressive statuary, including this monument to Bartholemeu Dias, first of the Portuguese navigators to round the Cape of Good Hope.*

ABOVE: *Among Strand Street's more prominent landmarks are the 18th-century Lutheran church, notable for its carved pulpit, and the adjoining Martin Melck House, which has been beautifully restored to its original condition.*

RIGHT BELOW: *Cape Town's Bo-Kaap, or 'Malay Quarter', on the slopes of Signal Hill, is home to a section of the city's Islamic community, many of whose members are descended from Indonesian slaves brought to the Cape during the 18th century.*

The oldest of Cape Town's buildings is the massive pentagonal Castle on which construction began in 1665 and ended eleven years later. For centuries the Castle served as the Cape government's military and administrative headquarters; it now functions largely as a museum which houses, among much else, the principal paintings of the noted William Fehr collection.

The Heerengracht, the city's broadest and perhaps most distinguished thoroughfare, sweeps up from the harbour towards Table Mountain to join Adderley Street, which is noted for its amiably raucous flower-sellers, its glittering arcades and malls, and for the Groote Kerk – a splendid Dutch Reformed church building of which the first stone was laid in 1700.

Strand Street is rich in history, with several buildings of the Dutch period still standing – of these the most notable are the Lutheran church, Martin Melck House and Koopmans-De Wet House. Adjoining Strand Street is Bo-Kaap, the picturesque tumble of narrow lanes, mosques and flat-roofed houses which is traditional home to a section of the Cape's Islamic community.

CITY
SQUARES

Of Cape Town's many and pleasant open spaces, Green-market Square is perhaps the most attractive. It is a bustling, cheerful place of street-traders' stalls, shoppers

and strollers. There are cobbles underfoot and the whole is garlanded by trees and girded by graceful buildings. One of the more notable of the latter is the Old Town House, an elegant mid 18th-century Cape Baroque structure once used by the Burgher Senate (the Dutch municipal council) and by the Burgher Watch, the city's first police force, and now in part a gallery housing some fine works of Dutch and Flemish art. Just across Burg Street is the Metropolitan Methodist church, a fullsome Gothic edifice regarded by Capetonians interested in the Victorian era as the country's most splendid house of worship.

A block or so away is Church Square, similar in proportion to Greenmarket Square but more sedate, providing access to (among other historic buildings) one of the entrances to the Groote Kerk. This church is distinguished by its magnificent pulpit, the work of the noted early sculptor Anton Anreith and the woodcarver Jan Jacob Graaff, as well as by its teak-and-pine roofing, vast roofspan and old gravestones, some of which have been incorporated as paving stones and others into the walls.

The Grand Parade is the largest of the city's open areas, originally used as a military parade ground and now forum for a lively open-air market and the occasional political rally. When Nelson Mandela was released from prison early in 1990, he addressed a huge throng of supporters from the balcony of the flanking City Hall, a handsome if rather elaborately Italianesque structure built in Edwardian times. The Hall's clock-tower holds a 44-carillon bell, the country's largest, and its auditorium is the venue for concerts given by the excellent Cape Town Symphony Orchestra.

ABOVE: *Greenmarket Square, at the heart of Cape Town, is one of the country's most charming plazas. Among its flanking buildings are the Metropolitan Methodist church (centre) and, in contrasting style, the Old Town House (left), meeting place of the 18th-century Burgher Senate.*

LEFT: *The Grand Parade, where the military once marched and drilled, now serves as the venue for a colourful open-air market. Fringing its southern perimeter is the old City Hall, designed in 19th-century Italian style, built of sandstone and completed in 1905.*

THE COMPANY'S GARDEN

One of Jan van Riebeeck's first tasks after coming ashore at Table Bay in April 1652 was to create a vegetable garden, one which would feed the Cape's first permanent European settlement and, perhaps more important to the Dutch East India Company's directors in Amsterdam, supply fresh produce to revive the scurvy-ridden crews of Dutch trading fleets on their long haul between Europe and the Indies.

LEFT: British sculptor Sydney Harpley's powerful – and controversial – statue of Jan Christaan Smuts stands at the southern end of the Garden. In the background are the twin towers of the Great Synagogue and, farther away, the Mountain's 'table cloth'.

That humble patch of ground still flourishes today, though over the centuries it has changed beyond recognition: it is now one of southern Africa's most attractive and botanically most interesting city parks.

During the 1680s a pleasure lodge made its appearance in the grounds, a structure that was rebuilt in elegant Colonial Regency style in the early 1800s and eventually became Tuynhuys, the Cape Town office of the State President. Both Simon van der Stel (who served as governor of the Cape from 1679 to 1699) and his son Willem Adriaan (1699-1707) enhanced and expanded the garden, the former allocating a section to the cultivation of rare plants, a function it still performs with distinction. By the beginning of the 18th century it had become a place of great beauty, a spacious expanse of greenery crossed by a broad avenue lined with lemon and orange trees, and by lesser paths fringed with pomegranate, quince, pear, apricot and apple.

Over the decades the garden's extent has been greatly reduced by the erection of several splendid buildings. Along Government Avenue, on the east side, stand the Houses of Parliament (completed in 1884, but added to several times since), Tuynhuys, the National Gallery, the Jewish Museum and Great Synagogue and Cape Town Commercial and Cape Town High schools. Opposite is Bertram House, the only surviving brick-faced Georgian house in Cape Town, and the Orange Street campus of the University of Cape Town. The South African Museum is an imposing feature of the western perimeter and the classically graceful South African Library, backed by St George's Cathedral, are on the northern side opposite Parliament.

More than 8 000 varieties of trees, shrubs and flowers, mainly exotic, can be seen in the gardens. In the centre there is a small aviary and a shady tea garden.

Oak-shaded Government Avenue is a favourite among Capetonian strollers, and home to an exotic species of tree squirrel introduced into the Garden by empire-builder Cecil John Rhodes.

The Whale Well is one of many splendid natural history exhibits housed in the South African Museum. Other sections are devoted to geology, archaeology and ethnology; of special interest are the displays of the Karoo's rich treasure-house of fossils.

CAPE TOWN HARBOUR

The city grew up around its harbour, though for nearly a hundred years after the Dutch settled at Table Bay the 'docks' amounted to no more than a simple wooden jetty, with ships at anchor in the bay loaded and off-loaded by lighter. In 1737 work started on a breakwater to protect shipping from the notorious Cape gales – the south-easters in summer and the even more destructive north-westers in winter – but it failed. In 1860 British Royalty in the person of Prince Alfred inaugurated a massive construction scheme that a decade later saw the completion of the inner Alfred Basin, which for the first time provided enclosed docking facilities, and in 1895 the outer Victoria Basin was completed. These two extensions enabled Cape Town to play host to the world's great merchant fleets, and to the Union-Castle and other well-remembered passenger liners that plied the seas in the era before travellers took to the air in numbers. In the years before, during and just after World War II huge quantities of sand were dredged to create Cape Town's Foreshore area, a 145-ha expanse of reclaimed land (now supporting broad thoroughfares and tall buildings) which made possible the construction of the massive Duncan Dock and Sturrock Graving Dock. In the late 1970s the present container berth was added.

Today the harbour is one of the best-equipped in the southern hemisphere, with 11 000 m of quayage, container terminals and huge floating cranes. Its grain elevator has a capacity of 27 000 tonnes and its pre-cooling stores and dry dock are among the world's biggest. It is an exceptional port in all respects – what irony therefore that maritime traffic has dwindled dramatically in recent years and that the docks have for many years been working to a small fraction of their capacity.

It is a sad decline, but for ordinary Capetonians perhaps a blessing in disguise, for their dockland is to serve a new and very exciting purpose. Vast and imaginative plans are under way to convert the historic Victoria and Albert basins into a prime recreational and tourist area with shops and fish markets, museums, hotels, restaurants and entertainment centres, promenades, a waterway leading to the city and a splendid yacht anchorage. It is sure to attract thousands of visitors and revive what has for many years been a dead area.

The Victoria and Alfred basins, oldest components of Table Bay harbour, are the focus of an imaginative and hugely ambitious waterfront development scheme. Seen here is part of the Victoria quayside and its clock tower.

THE NICO MALAN
THEATRE COMPLEX

The foyer of the Nico Malan's opera house is distinguished by massive chandeliers and richly-hued tapestries. Ballet, drama and orchestral concerts are also staged in the complex.

Opened in 1971, the 'Nico' as it is familiarly known to Capetonians, was South Africa's first major centre for the promotion of the performing arts. Situated on the Fore-shore (*see* page 19) and named after a former administrator of the Cape Province, the Nico is home to the Cape Performing Arts Board (CAPAB), which encompasses an orchestra and ballet, opera and drama companies.

The basic design consists of an opera house and a theatre, each with its own facilities and forming an L-shaped building which provides some shelter from the Cape's blustery south-easterly wind which prevails in summer. A much smaller theatre, the Arena, was subsequently added, mainly for intimate or experimental works. The overall impression on the visitor is a happy blend of grandeur and intimacy: immense chandeliers of Italian crystal light the opera house foyer, which is also hung with warm-hued

tapestries made in France to South African designs. Many walls are clad with marble, some from Carrara in Italy (the same used by the great classical sculptors) and some from the quarries of Namaqualand.

In the spacious auditoria, the sense of illusion – so essential to successful stagecraft – is aided by ingenious mechanisation and electronics. The main stage floors are set on lifts and include revolving stages. Backstage wagons carry pre-built sets, and utilizing a combination of these various aids, set-changing times are reduced to a minimum.

Tours of the Nico Malan Theatre Centre are conducted on Wednesdays and Fridays, and also on Mondays during December. The theatre is in production throughout the year, and in all some 100 ballet, 200 opera and nearly 300 drama performances may be staged annually, excluding children's theatre presentations held in the foyer during school holidays.

THE ATLANTIC SEABOARD

Cape Town's 'Riviera' extends along the Peninsula's Atlantic seaboard from Green Point and Sea Point south to Clifton and Camps Bay – a 10-km stretch of coastline characterized by rocky indentations, beautiful expanses of white sand and charming little embayments around which cluster some of the city's most fashionable residential areas. Behind them, looming over suburb and sea, are the imposing and often cloud-wreathed heights of Lion's Head and the first of the Twelve Apostles, both of which are extensions of the massive Table Mountain formation.

This is a prime holiday area, popular among leisure-bent Capetonians as well as out-of-town vacationers. The Atlantic waters here are too cold, really, for comfortable swimming, but in summer the backing mountains provide shelter from the prevailing south-easterly wind, and sun-worshippers are drawn in their thousands to the beaches. Of these,

Sea Point's beachfront promenade, seen here in the quiet hour after dawn. The inner suburb is one of Cape Town's more fashionable residential areas and, in summer, one of its livelier holiday spots.

the best are the four broad swathes of sand that grace Clifton's shoreline.

Sea Point has other enticements. It's a bright, busy, vibrant, cosmopolitan place of modern hotels and luxury apartment blocks, late-night restaurants, discos and delis. Along the elegant, palm-fringed and sociable beachfront, much favoured by evening strollers, are lawns and children's playgrounds and, towards the western end, one of the southern hemisphere's largest seawater swimming pools.

From Clifton and Camps Bay a spectacularly scenic highway twists its way southwards along the Peninsula's western coastline to Llandudno, a small, fashionable and exclusive village that hugs the precipitous slopes beneath a buttress called Little Lion's Head.

Beyond, over the spur and overlooked by the imposing peak known as The Sentinel, lies Hout Bay, an enchanting seaside town and fishing harbour nestling in a wide, green, hill-flanked valley. In translation the name means 'wood bay', a reference to its value as a source of timber in the earliest colonial days. The harbour now serves as the headquarters of the Peninsula's crayfishing fleet. Rock lobsters are not the only sea harvest gathered in by the local boats. In June and July huge quantities of snoek – a shoaling,

predatory fish which makes a delicious meal when smoked, salted or eaten fresh – are caught offshore and sold on the quayside. The annual and very popular Snoek Festival is held during this period. Here, too, is Mariner's Wharf, an emporium modelled on its famed counterpart in San Francisco. Live lobsters are sold here, as is the freshest of fish, and visitors are hosted in its atmospheric restaurant.

Hout Bay's other notable attraction is the World of Birds, a series of 'walk-through' aviaries quite beautifully landscaped to simulate natural habitats. Some 450 different species are in residence.

The marine drive continues over Chapman's Peak, a dramatic 10-km route slicing through cliffs that plunge to the sea 600 m below. From here the views of Chapman's Bay and, in the distance, Hout Bay and its distinctive Sentinel, are breathtaking. The road then descends into the flat, marshy plain of Noordhoek and farther along the shoreline reaches the pretty little coastal village of Kommetjie.

OPPOSITE: Fishing boats at rest on the still waters of Hout Bay's picturesque harbour. Crayfish and snoek are among the major catches, tourism a rapidly developing local industry.

RIGHT: *A tumble of villas and luxury apartment blocks decorates the slopes above the white sands of Clifton. Behind them, the hillside rises to meet Lion's Head, part of the Table Mountain massif.*

LEFT: *Hout Bay and its distinctive Sentinel formation, viewed at sunset from Chapman's Peak Drive. Beyond the mountains to the right are the forests and vineyards of Constantia.*

LEFT BELOW: *Chapman's Peak Drive, one of the Cape's most scenically attractive routes, cuts through different strata of granite and limestone, revealing multi-coloured rock faces. The cliffs fall almost sheer to the sea 600 m below.*

BELOW: *Noordhoek, a spacious residential area along the bay below Chapman's Peak, is famed for its broad beach and fine surfing waves, though the water here is usually too cold for leisurely bathing.*

FALSE BAY

'White as the sands of Muizenberg, spun before the gale,' wrote Rudyard Kipling. And the beaches along the Cape's False Bay coast are indeed white, and often uncomfortably wind-swept. The waters, however, are warm (the average summer temperature is 22° C), sparkling blue and a magnet for bathers, surfers, divers, skiers and yachtsmen.

Muizenberg, towards the southern end of the bay, is a somewhat old-fashioned town, noted for its turn-of-the-century villas and restored fishermen's homes. In Victorian and Edwardian times it was a famed seaside resort. Kipling loved the place and so did his friend Cecil Rhodes, who spent his last years in a cottage in nearby St James. Farther along the shoreline is Kalk Bay, one of the prettiest of the Cape's fishing villages, behind which rises a range of hills which, though modest in proportion, are remarkable for the number and variety of their labyrinthine caves.

Travelling south towards Cape Point, one passes through the substantial centres of Fish Hoek (one of the country's few 'dry' towns: no liquor may be sold within its bounds) and Simon's Town, which served as the Royal Navy's principal South Atlantic base from 1810 to 1957, when the dockyards were taken over by the South African Navy. The town is steeped in sea-faring tradition. Of special interest are the displays in its museum (formerly The Residency) and the Martello Tower, the earliest surviving British building on the subcontinent.

Beyond, virtually at the tip of Africa (only Cape Agulhas lies farther to the south), is Cape Point. This narrow, massive and high promontory is the finest of viewsites as its cliffs plunge almost sheer to the Atlantic Ocean 300 m below. It is off the Point that the *Flying Dutchman*, a phantom ship with broken masts and tattered sails (and reportedly sighted by many seafarers, including King George V when serving aboard a Royal Navy vessel in 1880), is destined to sail the southern seas until the end of time.

ABOVE: *Some of the finest of South Africa's beaches fringe False Bay's shoreline. Especially popular is Muizenberg's, seen here on one of its less crowded days. Bathing huts lend colour to the scene.*

BELOW: *Simon's Town, at the southern end of False Bay, was named after Governor Simon van der Stel, who explored the bay in 1687 and recommended it as a winter anchorage. The town has featured prominently in naval annals ever since.*

ABOVE: *The massive buttress of Cape Point, almost at the tip of Africa. Whale and dolphin, seal and tunny can often be seen sporting in the blue depths far below.*

GROOT CONSTANTIA

Originally designed and built by Simon van der Stel, the gifted early Cape governor and a man of impeccable taste, Groot Constantia is probably the finest of South

Africa's stately homes. Van der Stel lived there until his death in 1712. Later, in the 1770s, the estate became the property of Hendrik Cloete, who added a splendid spacious cellar and developed the vineyards to yield rich, sweet wines that were praised by poets and enjoyed by the royalty of Europe. Today the Constantia valley continues to produce excellent and greatly sought-after vintages, though no longer catering for those who like their wines sweet. The homestead, now a national monument, burned down in 1925 but has been exquisitely restored, its interior

ABOVE: *Early Cape furniture is a graceful feature of the Groot Constantia homestead. Other attractions include the two-storeyed, beautifully embellished wine cellar, and the wine museum.*

beautified by period Cape furniture and by some fine pieces of Delft, Rhenish, Japanese and Chinese porcelain.

Sharing pride of place with the homestead is the two-storeyed cellar. It is the work of the renowned French architect Louis Thibault, and its cherub-adorned pediment that of the sculptor Anton Anreith. Next door is a museum whose displays introduce the visitor to the intriguing world of wine and wine-making. From the homestead an oak-shaded avenue leads to the ornamental pool in which the Cloete family and their distinguished guests once bathed and where, it is said, the ghost of Van der Stel still lingers.

Groot Constantia is one of three wine estates enclosed by the valley. Nearby are Klein Constantia and Buitenverwachting, both of which have been lovingly renovated. The latter is noted for its stables and its slave quarters, and for its superb restaurant. Together, the three homesteads form the enormously popular Constantia Wine Route.

LEFT: *Groot Constantia, perhaps the stateliest of all the Cape's historic homes, stands among the vineyards of Constantia Valley. The estate's wines have been widely celebrated for almost 300 years.*

KIRSTENBOSCH

Beneath the spectacular eastern buttress of Table Mountain lies Kirstenbosch – peaceful, spacious and world renowned for its beauty. Kirstenbosch was founded in 1913 to preserve and propagate South Africa's magnificent floral heritage, and today serves as the headquarters of the National Botanic Gardens network. It also plays host to tens of thousands of visitors each year.

Here, on a 528-ha expanse of well-watered land bequeathed to the nation by Cecil John Rhodes, some 9 000 of the country's 18 500 species of indigenous flowering plants are cultivated, among them the proteas and ericas of the Cape Floral Kingdom's unique fynbos vegetation, pelargoniums (the stock from which geraniums have been bred), mesembryanthemums (or 'vygies', as they are called locally), disas and bulbs, succulents, ferns and cycads.

The displays are concentrated in some 40 ha of cultivated ground in a series of informally designed gardens graced

LEFT: *Kirstenbosch's spring annuals lend glorious colour to the slopes above Cape Town's southern suburbs.*

by natural features, terraces and rockeries. Part of Jan van Riebeeck's hedge of wild almond, planted in 1660 to keep the cattle of the Cape's first white settlement from straying, can still be seen on the estate. Of some historical interest, too, is the charming little sunken pool, lined with Batavian brickwork and shaped like a bird, that is known as Lady Anne Barnard's bath (though incorrectly so, as it was built by a Colonel Christopher Bird some time in the 19th century). In an amphitheatre on the slopes above the pool are the cycad plantings, one of the first collections to be developed. Nearby is the Compton Herbarium, repository for about 250 000 individual plant specimens.

Kirstenbosch is a place for all seasons, though it's probably at its most inviting during the months of September and October, when the spring annuals and many of the proteas are in glorious bloom. For visitors there are guided tours, an information office, a shop that sells seeds and souvenirs, a tea-room and delightful walks along many pathways. A 'braille trail' and a perfume garden in raised beds have been laid out for the blind.

ABOVE: *The giant or king protea* (Protea cynaroides), *South Africa's national flower and the largest of the genus's 83 members (it grows up to 30 cm in diameter), is one of 9 000 floral species cultivated at Kirstenbosch.*

GROOTE SCHUUR ESTATE

On the mountainside beneath Devil's Peak is Groote Schuur Estate, a large and lovely piece of land bequeathed to the nation by Cecil Rhodes on his death in 1902. Of the estate's several components, the sprawling, gabled mansion itself, also named Groote Schuur ('Great Barn'), is the most historic. It was originally a 17th-century granary, later converted into a house, which burned down and was then reconstructed for Rhodes by his friend and 'personal architect' Herbert Baker to serve as the Prime Minister's official residence. (It is now the State President's official residence.) Its spacious interior is distinguished by exquisite tapestries and a fine collection of English and Cape silver.

Nearby are Westbrooke, an elegant Edwardian house and

Rhodes Memorial with G.F. Watts's impressive statue of 'Physical Energy'. From here there are fine views over the suburbs to the sea, and towards the Hottentots-Holland Mountains.

today used as a State guest house, and The Woolsack, which once did duty as Rudyard Kipling's summer home and is now part of the University of Cape Town.

Students at the medical school of the University of Cape Town are trained at Groote Schuur Hospital where, in 1967, Prof Chris Barnard and his cardiac team performed the world's first human heart transplant operation. Also part of the estate is the university itself. The pleasant, ivy-covered campus buildings afford splendid views over the coastal plain to Table Bay and the Atlantic Ocean beyond. Higher up on the mountainside stands the Rhodes Memorial, a grandly imperialistic 'temple' built in neo-Classical style and incorporating two impressive pieces of statuary, namely G.F. Watts's 'Physical Energy' and a bust of Rhodes, beneath which is inscribed part of Kipling's moving tribute to the man and the 'immense and brooding spirit' he personified.

Other prominent elements of the Groote Schuur property include the paddocks, where antelope and a number of exotic species graze, among them Chinese deer and Himalayan tahrs or mountain goats; Mostert's Mill, a traditional Dutch windmill and one of Cape Town's best-known landmarks; and the Baxter Theatre complex, an integral part of the university. The Baxter is a major venue for experimental and indigenous drama, and for popular shows.

The University of Cape Town – the country's oldest, and perhaps its most attractive, university. The splendid heights of Devil's Peak provide the backdrop.

ABOVE: *Groote Schuur Hospital, set beneath the majestic heights of Table Mountain, has a proud place in medical history: it was here that the world's first human heart transplant operation was performed – in 1967, by Prof Chris Barnard and his cardiac team.*

LEFT ABOVE: *Part of the University of Cape Town's Baxter Theatre complex, venue for both popular and experimental music and drama.*

LEFT: *Mostert's Mill, one of Cape Town's best-known landmarks, faces onto the busy De Waal Drive freeway, just below the university campus. Built in 1796 as a 'horse' mill, it was carefully restored, with the help of the Netherlands government, in 1936.*

THE WESTERN CAPE

FRANSCHHOEK

Nestling in an enchanting valley among the mountains of the winelands, the town of Franschhoek was founded in 1688 by French Huguenot refugees who had fled a Europe torn by religious strife. They were independent people, proud of, and anxious to hold onto, their collective identity, but here at the Cape they were outnumbered by the resident Dutch and German 'free burghers' and were quickly assimilated, partly as a result of deliberate

PREVIOUS PAGE: *Boschendal estate in the Franschhoek area of the winelands, with the Franschhoek Mountains as a backdrop.*

ABOVE: *The lovely Franschhoek Valley, noted for its bountiful fruit orchards as well as for its vineyards and stately homes, many of whose names reflect their Gallic origins.*

RIGHT: *Franschhoek's graceful Huguenot Memorial, erected as a tribute to the late 17th-century French Huguenots, refugees from religious persecution, who settled, and enriched, the Franschhoek and Groot Drakenstein areas.*

policy. Within three or four decades they had ceased to exist as a discernible community.

These early immigrants did, however, bequeath some of their heritage to posterity. A number of them were skilled in the science of viticulture, and their expertise proved of enormous and lasting benefit to the local wine industry. They also exerted a powerful influence on the rural architecture of the pre-Victorian period. As their farms and those of their neighbours prospered, so they extended their modest homes, adding wings and cellars and gabled lofts, coach-houses, courtyards and slave quarters. By the early years of the 18th century a new, distinct and much-admired style – Cape Dutch – had begun to emerge.

Some of the most gracious of the Cape's homesteads are to be found in the Franschhoek ('French Quarter') and adjacent Groot Drakenstein areas, the names of many, such as La Motte, La Bri, La Provence, Haut Provence, Mouton-Excelsior, Les Chênes and more, reflecting their Gallic origins. Boschendal, an elegant Flemish-style mansion dating from 1812, is an especially fine example of the idiom. Long the property of the De Villiers family, it fell into decay during the latter part of the 19th century but has been lovingly restored and is now both a museum (exhibits include Ming porcelain) and the centrepiece of a splendid wine farm. The restaurant is renowned for its magnificent buffet spreads.

Franschhoek itself is a pleasant little town that serves the area's wine and fruit farmers. Its large but delicately graceful Huguenot Memorial, and the next-door museum complex, commemorate its founders.

The distinctive cluster of rounded peaks atop Paarl ('pearl') Mountain, centrepiece of the 2 000-ha Paarlberg nature reserve. The historic town of Paarl lies in the valley below.

PAARL

The three giant boulders of the buttress that soars high over the Berg River caught the eye of early Dutch explorer Abraham Gabbema when he saw it in the early morning, with sunlit dew glistening on its mica-studded surface. It reminded him of a 'diamant ende perel berg' (diamond and pearl mountain) and the image persisted, conferring a name on the lovely valley beneath, which became the Perelvallei (vale of pearls). Later the town that was founded there (in 1690) took the same name and became Paarl. The heights are now graced by a wild-flower garden and the surrounding slopes by a nature reserve in which aloes and wild olives, proteas and silver trees grow.

Paarl, the biggest of the western Cape's inland centres and one of the longest, with an oak- and jacaranda-lined main street that runs a full 10 km from end to end, began life as a farming and wagon-building settlement, later expanding its economic base to include quarrying, canning and manufacturing. The town is best known for its close historical associations with the Afrikaans Language Movement (it featured prominently in the campaign to have 'De Taal' recognized) and with the wine industry. The giant KWV organization, largest of the world's wine co-operatives, conducts its business from La Concorde, an imposing neo-Classical building on Main Street.

Just outside town is Nederburg, a large, gabled and quite enchanting homestead set in a countryside mantled by vines. In April each year the famed Nederburg wine auction is held here, an event known and enjoyed as much for its carnival atmosphere, culinary delights and fashion show as for its sales, which attract merchants, investors, collectors and serious wine-lovers from many parts of South Africa and, increasingly, from beyond the country's borders.

The graceful Taal (or Afrikaans Language) Monument on the slopes of Paarl Mountain.

Massive vats line the floors of the KWV's wine and brandy cellar complex in Paarl. KWV is the world's largest wine co-operative.

RIGHT: *Shaded by oaks planted by the early townsfolk, Stellenbosch's Dorp Street boasts the longest row of historic homes in the country.*

BELOW: *Situated on Die Braak (the village green once used for military parades and festivals) are several historic buildings which today form part of the town's museum complex.*

STELLENBOSCH

Set in the green and fertile valley of the Eerste River in the heart of the Cape winelands, Stellenbosch is South Africa's second oldest white settlement and one of the country's most historic towns. It was founded in 1679 as a farming centre and frontier village (at that time the colonists knew little of what lay beyond the mountains to the north) and named in honour of Simon van der Stel, the respected Dutch governor of the day.

The place grew with grace and dignity, distinction con-

ferred by avenues of oak trees planted by the early townsfolk and by the churches, schools and sturdy, thick-walled, thatch-roofed homes they built, designed to endure the passage of centuries. Today oaks still embower the thoroughfares, and much else of the past remains. The legacy is most clearly seen along Dorp and Church streets, around Die Braak (the green commonage once used for military parades and festivals, feasts and country games) and most especially in the Village Museum. This last is a magnificent

collection of houses dating from a number of eras, meticulously restored and furnished in period styles, their gardens planted with the same flowers, shrubs and trees that would have decorated the originals.

Stellenbosch is historically and intimately associated with the wine industry. Some of the Cape's most attractive vineyards and estates are concentrated along its Wine Route, and altogether there are twenty wine farms within a 12-km radius of town. All the estates and co-operatives on the wine route are worth visiting for their cellar tours and tastings, and many for the cuisine of their excellent restaurants, farm stalls that sell local specialities and the beauty of homestead and countryside.

In Stellenbosch itself, places of interest to the wine-lover include the Stellenryk Museum, housed in Libertas Parva, an elegantly gabled mansion which also serves as home to the renowned Rembrandt van Rijn art gallery; the Bergkelder ('mountain cellar'), carved out of the hillside and repository for an array of quite gigantic vats; the Oude Libertas brandy museum; and the Oude Libertas centre, whose extensive winery may be visited by appointment, and whose amphitheatre functions as an enchanting venue for open-air performances of drama, dance and music.

BELOW: *The VOC Kruithuis, or Dutch East India Company powder-house, built in 1777 beside the village green. It is now a national monument housing a small military museum.*

ABOVE: *The classically conceived Hoofgebou, the original building of Victoria College, predecessor of Stellenbosch University. The campus, academic home to some 14 000 students, is integrated into the charmingly tree-shaded town.*

ABOVE: *The amphitheatre at Oude Libertas, an enchanting venue for the open-air performances of music, dance and drama that are held on summer evenings.*

The Stellenbosch Wine Route encompasses 22 cellars and wineries, many attached to beautiful and historic homesteads. Here, visitors sample the excellent products of the Delheim estate.

TULBAGH

Earthquakes are a rare phenomenon in southern Africa, and when they do occur they're usually rather timid affairs, but on 29 September 1969 the Tulbagh-Ceres area, in the lovely wine and fruit-growing lands some 120 km north of the Cape Peninsula, experienced a tremor that measured a formidable 6,5 on the Richter scale. Great boulders were dislodged from the hillsides and clashed together in their tumble down the slopes to produce sparks that set fire to large parts of the countryside. Nine people died and many buildings were destroyed, among them some of Tulbagh's (and the country's) most time-honoured homes.

Tulbagh began life at the end of the 17th century when Governor Simon van der Stel visited, and was so entranced by, the green and pleasant valley that lies beneath the high Saronsberg, that on his return to Cape Town he persuaded a number of burghers to settle in the district. A congregation was established in 1743 and over the following decades the place grew, in unhurried and charming fashion, into a fairly substantial and delightfully picturesque country town.

After the earthquake Tulbagh's historic homes were me-ticulously restored and the 32 of them along Church Street combine to form the largest single group of national monuments in South Africa. The original church, which had managed to escape damage (though it had been suffering grievously from neglect), is now an integral part of the Oude Kerk Volksmuseum – a collection of four notable buildings that includes the Old Drostdy, once the residence and office of the Dutch East India Company's landdrost (or magistrate) in the region. This rather austere but impressive neo-Classical edifice, designed by the gifted French architect Louis Thibault, serves both as a museum and as the headquarters of a leading wine company. This hospitable firm entertains visitors to an excellent glass of sherry or its own Drostdyhof wine while they view works by local artists.

The Old Church itself contains 19th-century furniture and works of art by the painters Bowler and Baines. The Volksmuseum's other two components are The Victorian House (more period furniture) and Monbijou, also designed by Thibault and noted for its antiques.

The Oude Kerk (Old Church), built in 1743 and now part of Tulbagh's 'people's museum'. The complex also embraces the Drostdy, designed by the celebrated French architect Louis Thibault.

THE OVERBERG

Cape Agulhas, Africa's southernmost point, was given its name (which is derived from the Portuguese word for 'needles') by the early navigators when they found that here the needles of their compasses were unaffected by magnetic deviation. It is a modest feature, the unremarkable southern portion of a substantial inland plain that slips quietly under the ocean to become the Agulhas Bank, watched over by a splendid restored lighthouse (a national monument).

The nearest town of substance is Bredasdorp, notable as a wheat and wool centre, and for a museum that houses relics of many vessels wrecked along the rocky, gale-swept coast over the centuries, the most celebrated being H.M.S. *Birkenhead*, which came to grief off Danger Point 70 km or so to the west, in February 1852 with the loss of 445 lives.

The enchanting little harbour and fishing village of Waenhuiskrans, on the shores of Marcus Bay north-east of Cape Agulhas, takes its name from a huge sea-cave carved out of the nearby cliffs. To the early settlers this cavern seemed to be quite wide and tall enough to serve as a coach-house ('waenhuis') able to accommodate several wagons and their spans of oxen. The village's alternative (though unofficial) name is Arniston, which commemorates one of the most tragic maritime disasters to have occurred in these notoriously treacherous waters. On 30 May 1815 the British troopship *Arniston*, on its way home from Ceylon, was driven ashore by the south wind and a strong current, and foundered in the bay. Of the 378 people on board, just six survived drowning.

To the north-east lies the De Hoop nature reserve, one of the Cape's most important. Together with its marine section, it extends over 60 000 ha of endangered coastal fynbos (heath) vegetation and species-rich waters. The reserve is home to Africa's largest population of bontebok, and to 228 species of bird. Just to the other side of Arniston is the much smaller but just as pleasantly tranquil De Mond nature reserve.

ABOVE: *Fishermen's homes at Waenhuiskrans, a charming south-coast village that retains much of its 19th-century character. The shoreline here is notable for its strange rock formations.*

LEFT: *The finely thatched, white-walled cottages of Elim, a Moravian mission station established in 1824 to the north-east of Cape Agulhas. The village is one of the country's most picturesque.*

ABOVE: *The 18-million-candlepower lighthouse at Cape Agulhas, Africa's southernmost point. Here, the shallow continental shelf provides richly rewarding fishing grounds for commercial fleets.*

SWELLENDAM

The country's third oldest town, Swellendam had a stormy adolescence. Founded in 1747 in what was at the time the far-flung reaches of white settlement, it developed peacefully for a while and then, in 1795, declared itself independent of Dutch East India Company rule, the burghers complaining that they had 'for long enough been under the yoke of slavery'. (Ironically many of them were slave-owners themselves.) The 'republic' lasted just a few months, however, before submitting to the newly installed British regime later that year.

Swellendam rests in the tranquil valley of the Koringlands River that flows down from the Langeberg range in the Overberg region of the southern Cape, and is graced by some lovely old buildings. Of these, the most notable by far is the Drostdy (the early magistrate's residence), built in the town's first year and preserved as a structure of great charm and historical importance. It now serves as a museum housing period furniture, household implements, wagons and an unusual collection of early paper money. Other places of interest are the cluster of 18th-century craftsmen's premises nearby, the old prison and the next-door post office (the jailor was also the postmaster), the burghers' Oefeninghuis (a place for meetings and worship), and the Auld House, which belonged to the wealthy 19th-century 'merchant prince of the Overberg' Joseph Barry.

Just to the south-east of the town is the Bontebok National Park, established in the 1930s near Bredasdorp to the east but later moved to its present, more suitable location on the banks of the Breede River. The park was established on the initiative of a group of concerned local farmers, as by the 1920s only 22 examples of this sturdy, medium-sized antelope remained. In fact it seemed as if the bontebok would suffer the same fate as its now-extinct cousin, the bluebuck, that once roamed the Cape grasslands in large numbers. The park is now sanctuary to the country's second largest herd (smaller only than that in the De Hoop reserve: *see* page 48).

ABOVE: *These cottages and the threshing floor in the foreground are part of Swellendam's village craft museum which includes a blacksmith, a cobbler, a charcoal burner, a coppersmith, a miller and a cooper.*

RIGHT: *One of Swellendam's many fine 19th-century buildings, elegantly decorated with filigree cast-iron. The town is South Africa's third oldest.*

LANGEBAAN

Stretching south-eastwards from the splendid natural harbour of Saldanha Bay, about 100 km up the coast from Cape Town, is Langebaan Lagoon, a 16-km long inlet that serves as the focal point of one of the world's great wildfowl preserves.

The clear, shallow waters of the lagoon, the adjacent salt-marshes, the mud- and sandbanks, the islands and rocky shores of the bay attract an enormous number and variety of bird species: flamingoes, cormorants, gannets, herons, sanderlings, turnstones, gulls, ibis. Altogether some 50 000 individuals take up residence during the summer months, four-fifths of them waders. Curlew sandpipers are especially prominent: they and other migrants from the Arctic and sub-Arctic breeding grounds are drawn south to Langebaan Lagoon by the shelter it provides and by the rich abundance of marine algae, molluscs, crustaceans and other mud-loving creatures of this part of the western Cape coast. Schaapen Island, in the bay, is home to the largest known colony of southern blackbacked gulls.

The lagoon, the five offshore islands and around 20 000 ha

Springtime flowers carpet the countryside around Langebaan Lagoon, focal point of a magnificent wetland wilderness area, and of the more extensive West Coast National Park. The shallow waters are a magnet for tens of thousands of waders and other bird species.

of rather bleak, but in parts hauntingly beautiful, coastal terrain comprise the recently proclaimed West Coast National Park. The park is still under development and will become much larger once local landowners have been recruited to the conservation programme. A section of the park – the Postberg nature reserve – supports a modest game population of black wildebeest, bontebok and eland.

Other attractions offered by this part of the western Cape include the brilliant springtime flowers of the area, and the hospitality of its hotel, Langebaan Lodge, and nearby resort. The latter, Club Mykonos, is a large and lively leisure complex imaginatively designed in the Greek style to resemble a Mediterranean village complete with cobbled alleys, public squares and whitewashed, colourfully trimmed *kalifa*-type apartments.

NAMAQUALAND

The Cape's western parts, those stretching from a point 70 km beyond the Olifants River north to the lower reaches of the Orange, are known as Namaqualand. It is harsh country, sparsely populated, bleak and arid. There is practically no surface water, and the rains are less than generous, varying from 250 mm a year to a low 50 mm and even less in places. Often dense mists mantle the shoreline

and its hinterland when the coolness of the Atlantic Ocean meets and mingles with the warmth of desert air.

Most of this coastal strip consists of the Sandveld, a narrow belt of land distinguished by its 'raised beaches'. These are elevated sandy terraces, the legacy of a far-distant period when the surface of the sea was about 100 m higher than it is today. To the east of the Sandveld lies the broken country of the Hardeveld and beyond that the wastelands of Little Bushmanland.

On first acquaintance much of the terrain seems relentlessly forbidding, its vast emptiness incapable of sustaining any but the simplest, least appealing forms of life. Yet Namaqualand, and especially the Sandveld, is famed for its stunning profusion of succulents and flowering plants.

Namaqualand in springtime. The region, though barren-looking for much of the year, sustains an impressive 4 000 floral species which blossom in glorious profusion after the winter rains.

The region sustains over 4 000 floral species. Most are members of the daisy and mesembryanthemum families, but there are many others, including varieties of aloes, lilies and herbs. The small, low-growing plants are drought-resistant and the seeds lie dormant during the long dry months. Then, after the winter rains but before the onset of the desert winds, they must sense a warming of the earth and the imminent arrival of pollinators, for they burst into vivid life and mature in a matter of days to cover the countryside in glorious carpets of colour.

THE CEDERBERG

The magnificently rugged, 100-km-long western Cape mountain range known as the Cederberg takes its name from the rare and at one time practically extinct Clanwilliam cedar (*Widdringtonia cedarbergensis*) that grows in high places. These lovely, long-lived and once prolific trees suffered greatly from the woodman's axe and uncontrolled burning during the early years of white settlement. Happily, though, a few hardy specimens managed to survive the onslaught by clinging to the upper slopes, and these, now well protected, will be the nucleus of new generations.

The Cederberg is a vast, 71 000-ha wilderness area of lofty peaks, deep ravines, waterfalls, crystal streams, pools and

BELOW: *The 20-m high Maltese Cross, one of the Cederberg's many strangely-weathered rock formations. The range is named after the once-endangered Clanwilliam cedar tree.*

strangely eroded rock formations, many with highly descriptive names such as the Tafelberg and its Spout, the Wolfberg Arch, the 30-m cleft called the Wolfberg Cracks, and the stark, monolithic Maltese Cross.

Some 30 types of mammal have made their home in this wild place, including the agile klipspringer, the steenbok, the caracal, the shy bat-eared fox, the wild cat and the ubiquitous chacma baboon. More remarkable are the Cederberg's birds, and especially its raptors, king among which is the black eagle (*Aquila verreauxii*). Flora is rich and varied, sustained by generous rains and good soil. Gracing the slopes are rocket pincushions and red disas (*Disa uniflora*,

LEFT: *The rugged landscape of the higher slopes. The range is a paradise for the hiker, the climber, the photographer and nature-lover.*

ABOVE: *Another of the Cederberg's bizarre rock shapes is the Wolfberg Arch, viewed from a distance across the barren sandstone, copper-tinted by the sinking sun.*

commonly known as 'Pride of Table Mountain') and a myriad other species ranging from tough heath-type plants ('fynbos') and handsome indigenous trees to colourful spring annuals. Most notable of all, perhaps, is the exceptionally rare, pure-white snow protea (*Protea cryophila*), which lives precariously above the snowline and is found nowhere else in the world.

The Cederberg is criss-crossed by over 250 km of footpaths, and it attracts hikers, climbers, campers, bird-watchers, botanists, photographers and lovers of nature from far and wide.

THE SOUTHERN CAPE
& CAPE INTERIOR

THE GARDEN ROUTE

'The flowers grow there in their millions, the mixture of pleasant scents which arises from them, the pure and fresh air one breathes there, all make one stop and think that Nature has made an enchanted abode of this place....' So wrote a French traveller, in 1780, of that part of the southern Cape coast which today is known as the Garden Route, and which is scenically as lovely now as it was then.

The Garden Route is some 230 km long, extending from Mossel Bay in the west to Storms River in the east. On one

PREVIOUS PAGE: *Swartvlei is one of a chain of lakes in the attractive Wilderness area and is home to about 200 bird species, including 80 kinds of waterfowl.*

The southern Cape towns of Knysna and George are linked by a narrow-guage Class 24 steam train which carries passengers through enchanting countryside of fern forest and woodland.

side is the Indian Ocean, the shoreline a delightful compound of embayment, lagoon and river estuary, imposing cliff and golden beach, and on the other are the well-watered, densely wooded slopes of the Outeniqua Mountains, which in places rise to 1 500 m and more above sea level. The rains of the uplands are gentle, perennial and generous – the hills receive some 2 500 mm a year, more than enough to nurture the luxuriance of colourful plants and evergreen indigenous forest.

To the east are the Tsitsikamma Mountains, the name aptly derived from the Khoikhoi word for the sound of rain or running water. A 500-ha section encompassing some of South Africa's largest and finest natural forests has been set aside as a sanctuary for the stinkwoods, candlewoods, white alders, assegais and giant Outeniqua yellowwoods (one of which, the 'Big Tree', is over 42 m tall and estimated to be some 1 700 years old) of this region. Below the reserve is the Tsitsikamma Coastal National Park, an 80-km east-west strip that embraces the inshore waters of the sea, the cliffs of the shoreline and the narrow coastal plateau. The rugged and renowned Otter Trail passes through the park, and there is an underwater trail for swimmers and divers.

Knysna Lagoon – a popular venue for holidaymakers and renowned for the variety of its bird and marine life.

RIGHT: *Knysna Forest, part of South Africa's largest single expanse of indigenous high woodland. Among the tree species found here are the stately yellowwood and ironwood, the kammasie, stinkwood, white alder and blackwood. In its deep-green depths live the last, tiny and almost certainly doomed remnant of the once-great herds of Cape bush elephant.*

BELOW: *One of Plettenberg Bay's three golden beaches, with Beacon Island and its luxurious hotel and time-share complex in the background. 'Plet' is one of the country's most fashionable coastal resorts.*

LEFT: *The Storms River, a modest but attractive watercourse, rises in the Tsitsikamma Mountains and flows through the dense forests of the uplands before reaching the sea at the eastern end of the Tsitsikamma Coastal National Park.*

BELOW: *The Bloukrans River bridge, said to tbe the world's largest single-span concrete bridge, supports 451 m of roadway 216 m above the river.*

MATJIESFONTEIN

Some 250 km from Cape Town, just off the Great North Road that leads to Johannesburg and points beyond, is the perfectly preserved and quite charming little Victorian village of Matjiesfontein. The place is set, rather incongruously, in the arid bleakness of the Karoo, and was established and lovingly embellished by an imaginative 19th-century entrepreneur named James Logan.

Logan was a man with a liking for lonely places, a flair for business and a troublesome chest. He found that the crisp, dry air of the Karoo was kind to his lungs and decided to make both his home and his fortune in the area. He invested what little money he had in land (including that around Matjiesfontein's railway station), planted trees, sank boreholes to provide passing trains with much-needed water, and then opened a refreshment room for their passengers.

Finally, when the money began to accumulate, Logan built a grand hotel, naming it the Lord Milner in honour of the British High Commissioner of the day. By this time Matjiesfontein had gained fame as a health resort and was attracting a fashionable clientele that included Lord Randolph Churchill (Winston's eminent father), the Sultan of Zanzibar and the writer Olive Schreiner, who rented a villa and stayed long enough to complete *Thoughts on South Africa*, her most noted philosophical work.

The Lord Milner was completed in the early years of the Anglo-Boer War (1899-1902) and functioned for a while as a military hospital, its elegant turret being used as a look-out post. The village itself was the headquarters of the Cape Command and hosted some 12 000 British troops during the hostilities. After the war the hotel reverted to its peacetime role to become, and remain to this day, one of South Africa's finest country establishments.

The turreted splendour of Matjiesfontein's Lord Milner Hotel. The village, Victorian in every detail, has been preserved in its entirety as a 'living museum'.

OUDTSHOORN

Some of the most sumptuous of South Africa's Edwardian mansions are to be found in and around Oudtshoorn, principal town of the Little Karoo region of the Cape. They are the so-called 'feather palaces' – elaborately ornamented reminders of the sudden and fabulous wealth enjoyed by local farmers during the ostrich feather boom

RIGHT: *Steady demand for feathers (and for skins and meat) has assured the place of ostrich farming as a continuing feature of the Oudtshoorn area, where the only feather auctions in the world are held. Here, visitors to one of the show farms are entertained by an 'ostrich derby'.*

OPPOSITE: *A section of the Cango Caves' remarkable fantasia of dripstone formations. The largest of Cango One's 28 chambers is the Grand Hall, 107 m across and 16 m high. Botha's Hall contains a column fully 12,5 m high.*

that began in the later years of the 19th century, riding on a wave of fashion demand. The grandest of these homesteads was probably The Towers, a 20-room extravanganza of icing-sugar turrets, gables, cast-iron filigree, balconies and fanlights, teak panelling and white-and-gold French wallpaper. The feather industry declined dramatically after the outbreak of World War I, and Oudtshoorn slipped back into its historical role as a farming centre. Nonetheless, the breeding of ostriches continues to have a place in the region's economy, but today they are bred as much for their meat and skins as for their feathers.

Many of the mansions have been preserved, though they have been put to more functional uses. Especially notable

are Greystones, Welgeluk and Pinehurst, now a student residence. Shades of the past can also be seen in the town's museums. One of these, the house called Arbeidsgenot, was the home of the renowned Afrikaans writer, poet and politician C.J. Langenhoven (1873-1932), best known as writer of the poem that became South Africa's national anthem.

To the north of Oudtshoorn are the Cango Caves, one of the subcontinent's most splendid natural wonders. The vast underground limestone labyrinth of multi-coloured stalagmites and stalagtites, situated in the Swartberg range, were 'discovered' by a farmer in 1780, though implements and Bushman paintings show that they were occupied as early as the Middle Stone Age (8 000 to 2 700 BC). The 28 chambers, linked by 2,4 km of passages, as well as those of Cango Two (the beautiful 'Wonder Cave') and Cango Three (a 1 660-m sequence), are quite remarkable for the kaleidoscopic variety of their dripstone formations. Cango Four, recently revealed and still under investigation, lies beyond and lower down.

The complex is a prime tourist attraction. There are several other cave systems in the area, at least two of which are larger than Cango, but they are difficult to reach and dangerous to explore, and therefore are closed to the public.

THE VALLEY
OF DESOLATION

The gigantic cleft that slices through the Sneeuberg range just south-west of the historic town of Graaff-Reinet (*see* page 68) is aptly named, for the valley is indeed a desolate place, a barren moonscape of jagged columns and eroded rock formations remarkable for their bizarre variety. But they are impressive, even beautiful in their starkness, and they attract a great many visitors. The land here falls abruptly away from the high central plateau, and those who scramble up to the observation points are rewarded with stunning views. To the south rise the distinctive heights of Spandaukop and beyond lie the Plains of Camdeboo.

The Valley of Desolation lies on the south-western edge of the Great Karoo, a vast semi-desert area covering some 400 000 km² of the central and western interior. In geological terms the region is part of the Karoo System of shales and sandstone, layered in horizontal strata and resulting in terrain that is, for the most part, flat and featureless. In places the monotony is relieved by dolomite dykes (ridges) and sills (rocky outcrops) that have been thrust up by volcanic action over millennia.

This is a country of far horizons, of intense sunshine, bone-dry air, blistering days and freezing winter nights. Rainfall is low, varying from 375 mm a year in the eastern parts to less than 50 mm in the far west, yet the land is more bountiful than it appears to the casual observer. There is good underground water, and this is profitably tapped by wind-pumped boreholes. The Karoo's thousands of windmills and the sweet grasses (especially those of the eastern areas) sustain a large proportion of South Africa's 27 million head of sheep.

Despite the almost total lack of surface moisture, a surprising array of plants manage to survive and even flourish in the Karoo. Most of them are succulents uniquely adapted to the harsh environment, such as aloes, mesembryanthemums, euphorbias, crassulas and stapelias. Others are desert ephemerals – wild flowers whose seeds lie dormant for years but quickly germinate and blossom gloriously when the rare rains come.

The Valley of Desolation is the most notable feature of the Karoo nature reserve, a 16 000-ha wilderness area proclaimed to conserve some of this vegetation, and to serve as sanctuary for Cape mountain zebra and a number of antelope species indigenous to the region.

The dolorite columns of the valley, towering sentinels on the edge of the Great Karoo.

GRAAFF-REINET

One of southern Africa's most attractive and historic towns, Graaff-Reinet was established in 1786 within a loop in the Sundays River, in the foothills of the Sneeuberg range east of the famed Valley of Desolation. It is a graceful place of fine old homes, gardens, orchards and vineyards set oasis-like in the harshness of semi-desert. However, the quiet charm belies its turbulent early days: less than a decade after its founding the settlement's rebellious citizens drove out the Dutch East India Company's magistrate and declared an independent (albeit short-lived) republic. In the years that followed the British Occupation of the Cape in 1795, they stubbornly continued to challenge the authority of distant Cape Town.

Graaff-Reinet settled into a more respectable routine during the first decades of the 19th century and developed with dignity. Unlike most other South African towns, its growth

Drostdyhof, also known as Stretch's Court – a charming mall of flat-roofed Karoo cottages that have been combined with the Drostdy to form an unusual and very beautiful hotel complex.

was planned rather than haphazard and its streets were laid out to a careful pattern. A great many of its early buildings were built by especially talented craftsmen, and more than 200 of these have now been restored and proclaimed national monuments.

Of special note are Reinet House and the fine Drostdy. The former, a thatched and gabled Cape Dutch residence, was built in 1812 to a classic H-plan to serve as the Dutch Reformed church's parsonage. It was occupied for more than 80 years by the influential Murray family and now serves as a splendid period-house museum. In its garden grows what was (and probably still is) the world's largest grapevine. Before it was pruned in 1983 it extended over an area of 123 m² and had a girth of 2,3 m. The Drostdy, designed by Louis Thibault, is six years younger than Reinet House. It has been beautifully restored and, together with a mall of 13 renovated old cottages, now forms a rather unusual and very lovely hotel complex. Among the many other sites well worth viewing are the Dutch Reformed Mission church (now the Hester Rupert Art Museum), the stately Dutch Reformed church (modelled on England's Salisbury Cathedral), The Residency (a museum housing, among other things, a superb collection of sporting rifles), the Reinet Museum (known for its Karoo fossils) and the Graaff-Reinet Pharmacy (established in 1870, and still going strong).

Graaff-Reinet's Dutch Reformed Groote Kerk is a copy in miniature of Salisbury Cathedral in England. It houses an unusually fine collection of ecclesiastical silver.

THE AUGRABIES FALLS

At a point some 500 km from its mouth on the Atlantic Ocean, in a desolate land of sand, scrub and rock, the Orange River plunges thunderously into a massive ravine. These are the Augrabies Falls (the name is a corruption of a Khoisan phrase meaning 'big waters') and they are one of the great wonders of Africa.

At peak times the spectacle is breathtaking. When the summer rains in the far-distant upper reaches have been generous, the river's flow at Augrabies rises to over 400 million litres a minute, the waters descending through the nine-kilometre ravine in a tumble of cascades and racing rapids. At their most dramatic, they breach the rim of the main gorge in 19 different places to drop, sheer at first and then in a series of cataracts, to the turbulent, rock-enclosed pool fully 200 m below.

The Augrabies, ranked among the world's six largest waterfalls, is the centrepiece of one of South Africa's many national parks, proclaimed in 1966 to preserve 9 515 ha of land along both banks of the river. Recently a further 70 000-ha expanse, known as the Riemvasmaak, has been added to the park, enlarging it to the point where it can sustain black rhinoceros and other large game. Besides the rhino, species currently in residence include springbok, klipspringer, leopard, black-backed jackal, bat-eared fox, baboon and vervet monkey. Martial and black eagles are among the 160 bird species recorded in the area.

Despite the arid terrain, the region supports a remarkable variety of flora. Notable plants are the 'kokerboom' or quiver tree (*Aloe dichotoma*), camelthorn (*Acacia erioloba*), wild olive (*Olea africana*) and white karree (*Rhus viminalis*).

ABOVE: *The Orange River, at medium flood, surges through the 18-km-long Augrabies gorge on its way west to the Atlantic Ocean.*

69

KIMBERLEY

In July 1871 a small group of prospectors led by one Fleetwood Rawstorne stumbled across a scatter of diamonds in a hillock on the farm Vooruitzicht (owned by the brothers De Beer) some 30 km south of the Vaal River. Exciting finds had already been made at Klipdrift to the north and Jagersfontein far to the south-east, but Rawstorne's hill, known as Colesberg Kopje, proved to be the 'cap' of the world's richest known diamondiferous kimberlite pipe. It was swiftly demolished during the ensuing rush for wealth, the ant-like swarms of diggers working the ground ever deeper to create the famed Big Hole of Kimberley.

By 1872 the tents and shacks of the dusty, frenetic settlement housed some 50 000 people – a population second only to that of Cape Town. Mining conditions were chaotic. When Cecil Rhodes arrived on the scene later that year he found that some 3 600 individual claims were being worked, each a tiny nine metres square and most of them divided and subdivided into even smaller patches. Furthermore the great bowl of the diggings was criss-crossed by an intricate network of pathways which tended to collapse, especially in the rainy season. In due course, therefore, a cat's cradle of ropeways was used to convey the buckets of diamond-bearing earth to the surface.

Rhodes, and the lively young Cockney Jewish entrepreneur Barney Barnato, set about bringing some order to the diggings, steadily buying up the claims until they shared control of the entire field, the former through his De Beers Mining Company, the latter through his holdings in the Kimberley Mine. In 1888 Barnato sold out to his arch-rival for £5 338 650, at the time an almost unheard-of sum. The framed cheque now hangs in the De Beers boardroom.

Today, four of the pipes in the Kimberley area are still productive, though the Big Hole – until recently the largest man-made crater in the world – closed down in 1914, by which time it had reached a depth of 1 097 m and had yielded more than three tons of diamonds.

Kimberley itself is a substantial town of modern buildings and broad thoroughfares, though something of the atmosphere of its rugged heyday remains, evocatively evident in the sprawling, village-like mine museum. This comprises the Big Hole, the old headgear, a re-creation of river diggings and a collection of restored buildings. The country's only surviving electric tram runs between the museum and the city. (Interestingly, Kimberley does not derive its names from 'kimberlite' but from the first Earl of Kimberley who, in 1873, was British colonial secretary.)

LEFT: *The Big Hole, centrepiece of Kimberley's outstanding Mine Museum. The crater yielded a staggering three tons of diamonds before its closure in 1914.*

ABOVE: *Inside the diggers' pub, part of the Mine Museum. Among the museum's other components are the old headgear, Victorian cottages and shops, and Barney Barnato's boxing academy.*

THE EASTERN CAPE

& WILD COAST

GRAHAMSTOWN

The gentle, rather academic face that Grahamstown shows today's world is in striking contrast to its origins. The place began life as a garrison outpost in the troubled eastern Cape of 1812, and received its baptism of fire just seven years later. Though attacked by a 10 000-strong Xhosa

PREVIOUS PAGE: *Part of Transkei's magnificent, 280-km-long shoreline – a holidaymaker's and hiker's paradise. The ocean can be treacherous, though, and the coast is littered with shipwrecks.*

army, superior weaponry prevailed and the 350 defenders managed to hold out. Within 12 months most of the 4 000 or so British Settlers who landed at Algoa Bay in 1820 were allocated land in the area and many of these, ill-equipped to cope with the harsh realities of frontier and farming life, soon drifted into town.

Grahamstown then grew rapidly, and by 1831 it had developed into one of the colony's principal settlements, second only to Cape Town in size and importance. It also grew gracefully, as a high percentage of the British immigrants who had taken up residence were skilled artisans. What had once been an untidy encampment was transformed into an elegant little town of streets wide enough to enable ox-wagons to turn full circle, and of solid public buildings and charming houses. Some of the latter can still be seen, in their restored state, in a section known as Artificers' Square.

LEFT: *Grahamstown's Anglican cathedral of St Michael and St George, fringed on its southern side by handsome Victorian facades. The cathedral is one of 40 places of worship in the 'City of Saints'.*

Grahamstown is an attractive, bustling little city and a significant educational centre, home to a number of well-known schools and to the campus of the small, rather elite Rhodes University, intellectual heartland of English-speaking South Africa. The place also has an unusual number of churches, and for this reason is sometimes referred to as the 'City of Saints'. Dominating its skyline is the 46-m-high spire of the handsome Anglican cathedral of St Michael and St George. Other notable places of worship are the Wesleyan church, the Baptist chapel (1823) and St Patrick's Roman Catholic church, built in 1839.

Grahamstown's early residents are commemorated by the modern and impressive 1820 Settlers Memorial Monument, situated on Gunfire Hill next to historic Fort Selwyn. The complex is the venue for the annual and culturally important National Festival of the Arts.

ABOVE: *The 1820 Settlers Memorial is an extensive complex of exhibition halls, conference centre, auditorium, functions rooms, entertainment and recreation areas. Its showpiece is the Memorial Court, notable for its many symbols representing the British contribution to South Africa's cultural heritage.*

PORT ELIZABETH

The warm waters of the Indian Ocean wash the long, glittering beaches of Algoa Bay, stretching in a lazy arc from Cape Padrone in the east to Cape Recife with its towering lighthouse in the west. These early names were bestowed by pioneering Portuguese seamen, but the city itself was named after Elizabeth Donkin, wife of the acting governor of the Cape of Good Hope, who died tragically young in 1820. A memorial was erected in her name by her sorrowing husband in what is now the Donkin Reserve.

It was in that year that 4 000 British settlers landed at 'The Bay', where almost the only building was the sturdy stone Fort Frederick, built in 1799 to accommodate a 380-strong garrison. It is still standing and is, perhaps, the oldest building in the Eastern Province. Over a century later the arrival of the settlers was commemorated by the construc-

ABOVE: *The Pearson conservatory in St George's Park, the largest and most elaborate surviving Victorian conservatory in the country, is famed for its displays of tropical plants, and the nearby 28-ha park for its mature trees and massed annuals.*

LEFT: *This charming row of double-storeyed terraced houses, each with its shaded balcony, flanks Donkin Street on the northern side of the Donkin reserve. The terrace was built during the latter part of the 19th century.*

tion of the Campanile, 52 m high, with an unsurpassed view from a platform reached by a spiral staircase of 204 steps. From this prominent tower a carillon of 23 bells still rings out over a city which preserves many old and historic groups of buildings in such localities as Castle Hill, Alfred Terrace and Donkin Street.

It is this rich mix of old and modern that is one of the attractions of Port Elizabeth, where bustle is balanced by ready access to public parks and gardens. A palm-fringed stroll or ride by steam train along the beachfront at Humewood passes close by the world famous Port Elizabeth museum complex with its Snake Park, Tropical House for birds, Night House, and Oceanarium renowned for its performing dolphins. Nearby are lawns, gardens, tea rooms, tidal pools and warm sea-water baths.

ABOVE: *Port Elizabeth's Oceanarium is noted for its dolphins, caught in Algoa Bay and trained to play to the gallery. These three are a family: grandmother, mother, and baby (born just 24 hours before the picture was taken).*

ST FRANCIS BAY

Cape St Francis marks the western limit of St Francis Bay, a magnificent sweep of coastline extending 100 km to the east to Cape Recife (named in 1575 in honour of the patron saint of seafarers by the Portuguese navigator Manuel Perestrello). The bay's beaches are among the country's finest. Broad white sands and rolling breakers attract surfers of international class and wash ashore a huge number and variety of seashells belonging to both Indotropical and Cape temperate marine species.

The St Francis shoreline is segmented into a number of smaller embayments and their resort villages, the most prominent of which is Jeffrey's Bay. Here the surf is at its most challenging and the seashells unusually prolific and colourful. Searching the Jeffrey's Bay tideline is a favourite and rewarding pastime among holidaymakers; a museum in town houses some imaginative and quite enchanting shell displays. Among the other popular resorts are Schoen-makerskop, Seaview, Sardinia Bay, Aston Bay, the beautiful Paradise Beach, and Sea Vista, where villas and rather charming black-thatched chalets cluster around a marina.

Parts of the shoreline and its immediate hinterland have been set aside as conservation areas. Cape Recife nature reserve, close to the often crowded Summerstrand beach, protects the vulnerable dunes and bird life of the area. Seekoei River nature reserve is a bird sanctuary (its residents include redknobbed coot, little egret, wild swan and a number of tern species) around the common estuary of the Swart and Seekoei watercourses. Cape St Francis nature reserve is a tiny patch of fragile duneland close to the hamlet of that name. Other proclaimed land protects the natural bush vegetation of the region, and the Seaview game park hosts a variety of wildlife, including lion, cheetah, giraffe, zebra and kudu. Next door is a chinchilla breeding farm which welcomes visitors.

Seal Point, at the end of the St Francis promontory, is distinguished by its splendid lighthouse. The building stands 28 m high and its lamps generate 2,75 million candlepower.

Jeffrey's Bay, on the shores of St Francis Bay, is one of the world's most renowned surfing spots, attracting international competitors as well as large numbers of local surfers.

THE ADDO
ELEPHANT PARK

Part of Addo's 185-strong elephant population, flourishing descendants of a herd that had been reduced to just eleven animals.

Seventy years ago the thick, tangled vegetation of the Addo bush (in the Sundays River valley some 70 km north-east of Port Elizabeth) gave sanctuary to the last, tiny remnant of the once-great herds of Cape elephant and preserved them from extinction.

These destructively voracious creatures had been creating havoc in the cultivated lands of the region, and in 1919 the farmers finally lost patience. They called in a professional hunter, to exterminate them. About a hundred were shot, while the rest, a pathetic group of just eleven animals, escaped into forbidding bush country. An outraged public prevented further slaughter, and ten years later the area was set aside as a national park. By the late 1980s the Addo elephants (which are genetically identical to those of the eastern Transvaal lowveld, though only the males have

tusks and these tend to be rather short) had increased their numbers to a healthy 185, and survival was assured.

The Addo park covers some 9 000 ha of tough spekboom (*Portulacaria afra*) and other woody plants, acacia, grassland and Karoo scrub. Besides the elephants it supports numbers of buffalo, black rhino, eland, kudu and red hartebeest – about fifty mammal species in all. Some 170 resident bird species have been recorded.

Dense though the Addo bush is, visitors rarely have difficulty in locating and observing the elephants, as there are several game-viewing roads, and viewpoints have been established at watering places.

HOGSBACK

High in the Amatola Mountains, to the north of the small Ciskei town of Alice, is the scattering of cottages, holiday homes and three charming hotels known as Hogsback. The name is taken from the three mountain peaks that dominate this scenically spectacular part of the eastern Cape, and whose summit ridges vaguely resemble the bristle-backed wild hogs of the woodlands.

The Amatolas form the eastern end of the Cape's main coastal rampart. It is an imposingly high range, its slopes well watered and mantled by natural forests and exotic plantations. Run-off from the generous rains of the uplands flows into the Buffalo River, which winds its way across the Border region to enter the sea at East London, South Africa's only major river port. Loftiest of the mountain peaks are Elandsberg (2 017 m), Gaikaskop (1 962 m) and the triple peaks at Hogsback itself (1 937, 1 836 and 1 824 m). Tor Doon, which rises 1 565 m above sea level and from whose crest there are eagle's-eye views of the splendid countryside around, is a favourite with hikers and climbers.

The entire upland region is magnificent walking country. From some of the plateaux and forest openings you can see as far as the Great Karoo on the one side and the Indian Ocean on the other. The forest cover is dense, deep green and primeval, rich in stately yellowwood, white ironwood and Cape chestnut. The trees are girded by an underbush of *Rubus* bramble and an array of wild flowers that includes the exquisite hairbell (*Dierama* spp.). Here, too, there are cool mountain streams, clear pools, charming waterfalls and fern-fringed woodland pathways that take you to hidden and enchanted places.

Among the more pleasant of the shorter strolls is that leading from the village of Hogsback to the Oak Avenue site, a delightful retreat which serves as a venue for open-air interdenominational services at Christmas and Easter.

The Hogsback's forest cover, its fern-fringed woodland paths, wild flowers, waterfalls and breathtaking views entice hikers, ramblers and nature-lovers from afar.

EAST LONDON

South Africa's only major river port, East London was established in the 1830s at the mouth of the Buffalo River in the eastern Cape's Border region as a landing point for military supplies. It was known as Port Rex until 1848, when the area was annexed to the Cape Colony. Today East London is a major city in South African terms, being home to some 170 000 people.

Despite the town's strategic position astride the sea lanes, the harbour was slow to develop. Only in 1937, when the C.W. Malan Turning Basin came into operation, were liner passengers able to disembark directly rather than make their somewhat undignified way ashore by means of a wicker basket and lighter. The docks now boast some 2 600 m of quayside, a tanker berth, a container handling facility and a grain elevator with a storage capacity of 76 000 tonnes. The port handles some three million tonnes of cargo each year, most of it originating from or destined for the industries of the eastern Cape, Transkei and Ciskei. The harbour's major claim to notability, though, is the ingenious 'dolos' system used in the construction of the

Leisure yachts line the lower reaches of the Buffalo River, whose estuary provides the country with its only major river-port. Dredging, excavation and the erection of cleverly designed breakwaters have created an excellent anchorage.

breakwater. (The system comprises interlocking concrete units that together neutralize the powerful action of ocean waves.) The system was invented by East London engineer Eric Merryfield in 1961 and is now integral to harbour design throughout the world.

East London is a major tourist centre. The town itself has three superb beaches, of which Orient is the closest and most popular. The excellent local museum is doubly distinguished: it displays the world's only known dodo's egg (the last of these Mauritian flightless birds, *Raphus cucullatus*, died in about 1680), and the first coelacanth to be caught in modern times and identified as such. The fish, a 'living fossil', was previously thought to have become extinct some 60 million years ago, but a specimen caught not far from East London's shores in 1938 proved otherwise.

THE WILD COAST

One of the most beautiful of the world's shorelines runs from the eastern Kei River (western limit of the Cape Province) to the Mtamvuna River bordering Natal. This 250-km expanse of unspoilt wilderness is famed for its scenic variety, sandy bays, lagoons and estuaries, imposing cliffs and rocky – and, for passing ships, notoriously trea-cherous – reefs that probe finger-like out into the warm, intensely blue waters of the Indian Ocean. The hinterland is just as attractive in its own way: here there are undulating hills, dense woodlands and a myriad streams and rivers.

This is the Wild Coast of Transkei, historic homeland of sections of the Xhosa people, and increasingly a magnet for leisure-bent visitors. Yachtsmen, anglers, golfers, hikers, cam-pers, bathers, surfers, skin-divers and lazers in the sun all find it a most congenial area. Gamblers do, too, for the Sun Inter-national group chose an especially attractive section of the coast as the site for one of its more splendid hotel-casinos.

Numerous smaller beach- and river-mouth settlements have been established along the Wild Coast. The largest of the seaside villages is Port St Johns, a sleepy little place in a magnificent setting of mountains, soaring cliffs and wide, golden beaches. Its river, the Mzimvubu, is navigable for some ten kilometres, and pathways lead through the sub-tropical forest to secluded and enchanting beauty spots. Among other noted resort areas are Coffee Bay, Umnagazi River (the lagoon here is much favoured by fishermen), Qolora Mouth (close by the lovely pool where the prophe-tess Nongqawuse experienced her fatal vision) and Mazep-pa Bay. This last is distinguished by its palm-fringed beaches and a hotel renowned for the seafood it serves.

Probably the most distinctive of the Wild Coast's natural features is a detached cliff that stands island-like in the sea, and through whose huge arched opening the surf thunders. This extraordinary structure is known to the local people as esiKhaleni, which means 'place of the noise', and to visitors as the Hole in the Wall.

Hole in the Wall – an arched opening through the massive bulk of a detached cliff – is one of the Wild Coast's best known and most photographed features. Its flat top is extensive enough to accommodate several soccer fields.

Natal

THE SOUTH COAST

The coastline stretching 300 lovely kilometres south from the city of Durban to the Transkei border is generally acknowledged as one of the southern hemisphere's most entrancing holiday regions, drawing tens of thousands of holidaymakers to its shores each year. Its attractions are a balmy tropical climate; broad, golden expanses of beach; the warm waters of the Indian Ocean; a lush, evergreen hinterland; fine hotels, and a score or more of pretty little resort towns, villages and hamlets that hug the shores of bays, blue lagoons and estuaries.

Each resort has its distinctive personality, but all offer sun, sea and sand; safe bathing (shark nets protect the swimmers); surfing; rock, surf and deep-sea fishing; sailing and the full complement of watersports. The largest of these centres are Amanzimtoti, 25 km from Durban; Scottburgh

(known for its fine golf course, an especially charming miniature railway, and 'Crocworld', which offers numerous wildlife attractions); Port Shepstone, at the mouth of the Umzimkulu River – largest of southern Natal's watercourses – has a welcoming country club and superb golfing facilities; and, busiest of all, Margate, named after, and in many ways much like, the popular English seaside town.

Some 20 km inland from Port Shepstone is the 2 000-ha Oribi Gorge nature reserve, of which the centrepiece is a spectacular canyon carved through the sandstone by the Umzimkulwana River. The gorge is 24 km long, 5 km wide and 366 m deep, and the vistas are breathtaking. The reserve's wildlife includes about 270 bird species and 40 kinds of mammal. However, the graceful and now rare oribi, from which the gorge and reserve take their name, no longer inhabits the area.

PREVIOUS PAGE: *Carved by the Umzimkulwana River, the Oribi Gorge is one of Natal's most outstanding beauty spots.*

BELOW: *Uvongo, at the mouth of the Vangu River, is one of many secluded resort areas on a coast blessed by a balmy tropical climate, golden beaches and a lushly green hinterland.*

THE VALLEY OF A THOUSAND HILLS

The most distinctive natural feature of the hinterland west of Durban is the hill-studded valley that follows the course of the Mgeni River from a strikingly prominent, flat-topped height called Natal Table Mountain to the Indian Ocean, a distance of some 65 km. The mountain rises nearly 1 000 m above sea level, and its plateau-like summit, reminiscent of the famed Cape landmark of the same name, is notable for the profusion of its wild flowers and the magnificent vistas that reward those who make the climb

ABOVE: *An impressive vista of the valley and its flanking hills. Two of South Africa's biggest and most exhausting sporting events – the 'Dusi canoe marathon and the Comrades marathon – take place in the area.*

to the top (the best route up starts from the Pietermaritzburg side). At the base of the massif is Nagle Dam, a significant reservoir that doubles as a recreational area.

The valley itself is uncomfortably hot in summer, but the scenic route leads you along the higher, cooler parts. The drive is well worth undertaking for the rugged and beautiful landscapes that unfold and for the richness of the plant life. Prominent within this floral kaleidoscope are arum, fire and snake lilies, red-hot pokers, Mexican sunflowers and colourful aloes.

The area is occupied by the Debe people (an Nguni group), many of whom live in traditional 'bee-hive' huts and some of whom still wear traditional dress. A more comprehensive, if rather contrived, insight into 'authentic' Africa is provided by the valley's pheZulu enterprise, a complex comprising a Zulu village, art gallery and shop. On offer here are demonstrations of Zulu dancing (a memorable spectacle), African cooking, thatching, beading and spearmaking. Somewhat similar is the Assegai Safari Park, but there is also a charming botanical garden, a natural history museum and enclosures filled with about 400 crocodiles and other reptiles. Also worth visiting is the Umgeni River Bird Park. Rated among the world's top three avian sanctuaries, its walk-through aviaries contain some 300 exotic and indigenous species.

DURBAN CITY

South Africa's third city, leading seaport and premier holiday playground was founded by a small group of English traders and hunters in the 1820s and grew up around one of the southern hemisphere's most splendid natural harbours. Today, 300 km² in area, the city sprawls along magnificent Indian Ocean coasts to the north and south, and inland to and over the slopes of the Berea, a semi-circular ridge of hills overlooking the skyscrapers of the central business district, the elegant beachfront and the bay. At the top of the ridge is the local campus of the University of Natal. Beyond, to the west, is a plateau high enough for the residents of its fashionable suburbs, such as Hillcrest and Kloof, to escape the worst of Durban's notorious summer heat and humidity.

The Berea and the bay are the city's most distinctive topographical features. The latter is a vast, more-or-less landlocked lagoon, its southern waters bounded by an eight-kilometre-long wooded headland known as The Bluff, its northern waters by a narrower, sandy spit called The Point. The harbour handles more than 30 million tons of cargo (mainly sugar, fruit, maize, coal, oil, manganese and manufactured goods) a year.

In some respects Durban is a very English city and indeed its 19th-century colonial white citizens were counted among Queen Victoria's most loyal subjects. Today, however, people of British stock are in the minority in the greater metropolitan area. The place is home to large numbers of Indians, some of them direct descendants of the indentured labourers persuaded to come from India during the 1860s to work the new sugar plantations of the hinterland. These Asian communities, many of whose members are now prominent in local industry and trade and in the professions, have cherished their natural heritage and have retained their religions, languages, customs, music, dress and cuisine. They add colour, character and vibrancy to the city scene.

Even larger is the black community. Durban is said to be the world's fastest-growing conurbation, its population expanding perhaps more explosively than that of Calcutta or Mexico City, and for much the same reason: the armies of the poor are leaving a countryside that can no longer meet their minimum needs, and are congregating in their tens of thousands in ramshackle settlements on the city's western fringes. Their integration into the urban mainstream is the challenge of the future.

Durban's magnificent harbour. The 900-ha bay is one of the very few natural anchorages on the Natal coast, though large vessels only gained entry at the end of the 19th century, after decades of dredging.

LEFT: *Just south of Durban's central business district, in Grey Street, stands the southern hemisphere's largest mosque. An imposing affair of golden domes, it is one of the many places of worship that serve Durban's industrious Indian community.*

LEFT BELOW: *The Workshop in Pine Street, a vast Victorian building that once served as a railway workshop and recently was transformed into a lively shopping complex and 'theme centre'.*

BELOW: *The Da Gama clock on the Victoria Embankment commemorates the first European sighting of the Natal coast – by the Portuguese navigator Vasco da Gama, on Christmas Day 1497.*

THE GOLDEN MILE

Durban's beachfront has been a prime tourist attraction since the first land-locked Transvalers began entraining south for their annual holidays in the later years of the 19th century. By the 1960s, however, it was sorely in need of a facelift, and the City Fathers decided on a massive redevelopment programme. The result was the 'Golden Mile', a stretch of beachfront that contains, along its six

kilometres, just about everything the hedonist could wish for. It is an extravaganza of sound and light, of wide white beaches, emerald lawns, fountains, graceful walkways and broad thoroughfares that lead past some of the country's most modern hotels, as well as pavilions, pools and amusement parks, emporiums and markets, night-spots, entertainment centres and round-the-clock eateries.

But the Golden Mile does have its more serious elements as well. Seaworld, for instance, is part of a non-profit-making organization devoted to the examination, preservation and intelligent use of the oceans's resources. Here dolphins, seals and penguins are bred under scientific conditions, injured marine mammals are treated and the many creatures of the sea are studied. The money generated by Seaworld's renowned aquarium and dolphinarium helps pay for the research. Similar in intent is the Fitzsimons Snake Park, which houses about 80 of South Africa's 157 snake species and an intriguing array of other reptiles such as crocodiles, leguans (iguanas), turtles and tortoises.

Ranking high among the Golden Mile's other attractions are the lawns, sunken gardens and summer houses of The Amphitheatre, a pleasant retreat from the bustle and noise of the holiday mainstream, the decorative rickshas (light man-powered carts) that have given joy-rides to generations of visitors, and The Wheel, one of the newest and liveliest of Durban's shopping and entertainment complexes. The latter takes its name from a giant and unashamedly garish Ferris wheel mounted on the building's facade (above a jewel-encrusted elephant's head) and girded by Indian howdah gondolas. Inside the theme is part Oriental, part nautical, and there are restaurants, bars, a dozen cinemas and about 140 speciality shops.

Marine Parade, part of Durban's Golden Mile – a 6-km-long stretch of developed shoreline that contains just about everything the leisure- and pleasure-bent visitor could wish for.

THE ST LUCIA COMPLEX

Zululand's Lake St Lucia is the centrepiece of one of the largest and most remarkable marine wilderness areas in Africa, an intricate complex of lagoons, rivers, lily-covered pans, game reserves, coastal forests, sand-dunes and sea.

The lake itself is 36 000 ha in extent and was formed 60 million years ago when the ocean receded to leave a sandy flatland, parts of which lay low enough to retain both sea and fresh water in a series of lagoons stretching up from the mouth of the Mkuzi River. The waters, 20 km wide in the north, are shallow (the average depth is about a metre) and home to some 600 hippos, crocodiles and huge numbers of fish, crustaceans, insects and other edible creatures that attract a stunning variety of birds such as flamingoes, saddlebills, Caspian terns, 12 species of heron and thousands

upon thousands of white pelicans. There is also a breeding community of African fish eagles.

Among the complex's other components are the St Lucia park, a belt of proclaimed wildlife preserve covering most of the lakeshore, the dunes and woodland of the Cape Vidal state forest, where rhino, buffalo and kudu can be seen, the dense and beautiful Dukuduku forest reserve, the Eastern Shores nature reserve, and the St Lucia and Maputoland marine reserves that extend across 88 000 ha to the Mozambique border. Offshore there are coral reefs that offer splendid opportunities for big-game fishermen.

Plans are under way to consolidate and expand all this protected land to create a vast, 275 000-ha Greater St Lucia Conservation Area that would rank among the great wonders of wild Africa. Two of the components have, however, been under serious threat, namely the Dukuduku forest (from the encroachment of homeless squatters) and the ecologically fragile Eastern Shores (from a scheme to mine titanium-bearing sand, which was shelved following a public outcry).

ABOVE: *Part of the St Lucia wetlands, one of Africa's largest and most remarkable wilderness areas.*

THE UMFOLOZI GAME RESERVE

The Umfolozi and its renowned companion, the Hluhluwe, are among Africa's oldest game sanctuaries, having been founded in 1897 – the former among the green hills and floodplains between Zululand's White and Black Mfolozi rivers, the latter some distance to the north-east. There are plans to consolidate the two in order to create a wilderness complex that will rival the Kruger National Park in size and even exceed it in the wealth of its wildlife.

The Umfolozi's warm, well-watered 48 000 ha were home to teeming game populations long before man's permanent presence. Then, during the early 1900s of the 20th century, farmers began to settle the region, and in due course they introducing livestock onto their lands, a move which was to have disastrous consequences for the wild animals. In the 1920s, in an ill-conceived effort to eradicate tsetse fly and the deadly nagana cattle disease it bore, the authorities inaugurated a massive game extermination programme. More than 100 000 head were slaughtered before its futility was acknowledged in 1945 and the killings abandoned in favour of chemical controls.

The reserve made an excellent recovery, and today serves as haven for dense concentrations of buffalo and elephant, giraffe, zebra, a wide variety of antelope, lion, leopard, cheetah, wild dog, hyena and white rhino (*Ceratotherium simum*) which had once grazed on the sweet grasses of the area in impressive numbers.

The rhino, indeed, is probably the principal character in what is generally held to have been a stunning ecological success story. The species – vulnerable to habitat change and prime target of hunters – faced almost certain extinction until, in the 1960s, Natal Parks Board rangers launched an ambitious and deservedly well-publicized rescue operation which captured world headlines. These animals are still on the endangered list elsewhere but now thrive in the Umfolozi. The reserve holds about 1 000 of them, and surplus head are regularly translocated to other parks throughout and beyond South Africa.

The area is a vital breeding ground, too, for the white rhino's threatened smaller cousin. Two decades ago the continent-wide population of black rhinoceros (*Diceros bicornis*) stood at over 60 000; by the mid-1980s fewer than 4 500 remained, of which 400 were to be found in Natal. The Umfolozi is one of the keys to their survival.

One of the Umfolozi's white rhino. The species, and its black cousin, have been saved from the brink of regional extinction; the reserve now holds some 1 500 of the animals.

Pietermaritzburg is famed for its lovely salmon-coloured buildings, one of which is the City Hall. Completed in 1893, it is said to be the southern hemisphere's largest all-brick edifice.

PIETERMARITZBURG

The noted traveller H.V. Morton once wrote that Pietermaritzburg 'wears its air of grace and quality with becoming ease', which was both an elegant compliment to and an accurate observation on Natal's capital and second city. The place does indeed have a quiet quality about it, discernible in its lovely salmon-coloured Victorian buildings, old-fashioned store-fronts, cast-iron railings, bookstores and antique shops that are everywhere, and in gardens luxuriant with roses and azaleas.

Although founded by the Voortrekkers in 1838, Pietermaritzburg is essentially a colonial city, English in character and, by tradition, in loyalty as well. It served as administrative centre of the Crown Colony of Natal from 1857 until 1910, when the Act of Union created a modern South African state, which many Natalians found hard to accept.

Much of the pre-Union heritage remains, seen at its best perhaps in the handsome Assembly buildings and the massive and elaborate City Hall, both completed in 1893, the year Natal was granted responsible government. The latter building, the southern hemisphere's largest all-brick edifice, is notable for its domes, stained glass and grand clock-tower. Another notable brick building is the gracious pavilion in Alexandra Park, a reminder of the gentler days of sporting competition.

Among the many other historic sites are Palmdene House, magnificently restored and distinguished by its cast-iron-work; Fort Napier and its garrison church, sited imposingly on a hill overlooking the city; the Old Supreme Court, and the Anglican Church of St Peter, consecrated in 1837 and scene of lively religious controversy in the 1860s, when Bishop Colenso challenged orthodox precept.

Evocative, too, are the Central Lanes, a charming network of narrow pedestrian alleyways that once served as the hub of Pietermaritzburg's financial and legal life. They encompassed four different stock exchanges between 1888 and 1931 and, because of the Supreme Court's proximity, an unusual number of lawyers' chambers. Of special interest to visitors are the Lanes' small speciality shops and the enchanting Edwardian Harwin's Arcade.

The charming pagoda-style pavilion in Alexandra Park, a 65-ha oasis that encompasses bright displays of azaleas, bougainvilleas and roses, as well as numerous sport venues.

THE HOWICK FALLS

The Mgeni River tumbles over a number of splendid waterfalls on its swift course through the Natal Midlands. The Shelter, the Cascade, the Albert, the grand 105-m-high Karkloof, each has its own distinction – but ranking above all in grace and splendour is the one known to the local population as kwaNogqaza, which means 'place of the tall one'. Europeans call it the Howick. It plunges over the rim in a single sheet of water to fall sheer for 95 m in a setting that is almost tropical in its deep green luxuriance. The cataract and 32 ha of the surrounding area have been declared a national monument. An observation site is located just above the waterfall and a steep pathway descends to the river bed below, from where there are different but equally enchanting views.

Farther upstream the Mgeni has been contained to create the Midmar Dam. Surrounding it is a public resort and nature reserve, a 2 800-ha recreational area popular among Natalian weekenders, water-sportsmen, bathers (the water is free of the bilharzia snail) and anglers (carp and bass are among the catches). Here, too, is the Midmar Historical Village, which features among other things a traditional Zulu homestead, a wood-and-iron Hindu temple, a blacksmith's shop, and the retired steam-tug *J.E. Eaglesham*, now moored in the dam's fresh water after occupying an honourable working berth in Durban harbour for many years. Denizens of the adjacent game park include white rhino, zebra and various antelope species.

Close to the waterfall is the town of Howick, a bustling, attractive centre named by the distinguished 19th-century British statesman Earl Grey after his stately home in Northumberland. Among the local hostelries is the historic Howick Falls Hotel, which has been in business since 1872 and which, in its early days, played host to the eminent Americans Mark Twain and the newsman-explorer Henry Morton Stanley.

ABOVE: *The 95-m drop at Howick down which the Mgeni River plunges on its rapid race through the Natal Midlands.*

RORKE'S DRIFT

On 22 January 1879 a magnificently disciplined, 17 000-strong Zulu impi descended on a British army encampment beneath the hill of iSandlwana, close to the border between Natal and Zululand. Surprise was complete, the battle short, bloody and conclusive: the British force was annihilated. Eleven kilometres to the west a small garrison at Rorke's Drift learned of the disaster from two fleeing survivors, and prepared to meet the expected onslaught.

Rorke's Drift, a ford across the Buffels River, was the site of a trading store until 1878, when the Swedish Missionary Society took over the place and expanded it. At the outbreak of the Anglo-Zulu War a year later the station – a modest cluster of two stone buildings, a chapel-cum-storeroom, a mission house and a cattle kraal – functioned as a British military hospital and commissariat depot under the command of Lieutenants John Chard and Gonville Bromhead. The garrison totalled 110 men, while 35 others lay sick in the chapel.

By mid-afternoon on the 22nd, just a few hours after the field of iSandlwana had fallen silent, some 4 000 Zulu warriors were gathered on the slopes above the now-barricaded outpost (loop-holes had been driven into walls and a barrier of biscuit-boxes, mealie-bags and two sturdy wagons hastily erected). At 16h30 the impi attacked, and continued to do so throughout the night in a superb sustained show of courage – but without success. When it finally withdrew at dawn, it left 350 of its dead behind. British casualties numbered 17 killed and ten wounded.

Rorke's Drift has gone down in the annals as a glorious feat of arms. It was certainly considered so at the time: a total of eleven Victoria Crosses were awarded for gallantry during the action.

The battle-ground remains very much as it was a century and more ago. The old buildings are still there and the river, ford and hills around are unchanged. A mission continues to function, and a craft centre where tapestries, hand-woven rugs, printed fabrics and pottery are made is a colourful addition to the scene.

RIGHT ABOVE: *The present mission station, close to the site where, on 22 January 1879, bloody battle was joined by Zulu and Briton. The small stone obelisk commemorates the 17 British dead; some 350 Zulu warriors were also killed.*

RIGHT: *One of the attractively colourful tapestries woven by the craft centre that now flourishes at Rorke's Drift.*

The view from the bottom of Sani Pass, the only transport route across a 250-km stretch of the high mountain barrier, beyond which lies Lesotho.

THE DRAKENSBERG

The massive chain of heights called the Drakensberg (the 'Dragon's Mountain') is the most splendid and prominent segment of the Great Escarpment, a sequence of ranges that runs down, across and then up southern Africa's U-shaped perimeter rather like a gigantic horseshoe, dividing the narrow coastal plain from the subcontinent's high interior plateau. The sequence is at its loftiest in the kingdom of Lesotho, where it is known as the Maluti Mountains, but in visual terms is most spectacular in the east, where the heights plunge, almost sheer, a full 2 000 m to the green and pleasant countryside of the Natal midlands.

Geologically speaking the Drakensberg is a young mountain range, formed barely 150 million years ago by seismic

The Tugela River, South Africa's third-ranked watercourse, on its initial 600-m plunge down the escarpment's precipitous eastern face.

convulsions that covered the sandstone plains with gigantic deposits of basalt lava. The 'wall' so created – 200 km wide, 4 000 m above sea level – was then, over the millennia, eroded by river and rain, elements that carved the deep ravines and sculpted the Drakensberg's remarkable fantasia of buttresses, dragon-tooth ridges, cliffs, caves, ledges and balancing rocks. The peaks and massifs have evocative names such as The Amphitheatre, The Sentinel, Mont-aux-Sources, Devil's Tooth, Champagne Castle, Cathkin Peak, Giant's Castle, Cathedral Peak and The Organ Pipes. To climbers they are a magnificent challenge and to the ordinary visitor they represent the ultimate in grandeur.

The 'Berg has a lot to offer the holidaymaker. Those drawn to the gentle foothills where a large number of resort hotels have been established come for relaxation in a casual and

Bushman (San) cave paintings are a striking feature of the Drakensberg region. Some, like these, may be seen in the Giant's Castle reserve, within which there are two site museums.

sociable environment, fresh, clean mountain air, rambles and hikes and horseback rides, the trout in the streams and the animals in the reserves. Of the latter, two are especially notable: the Royal Natal National Park, an 8 000-ha wilderness of unparalleled scenic beauty, and the Giant's Castle nature reserve, which sprawls over 35 000 ha of rugged mountain terrain famed for its bird life (among its resident raptors are martial, crowned and snake eagles and lappet-faced, hooded, whitebacked, Cape and bearded vultures). Both these parks are graced by some of the region's finest 'galleries' of Bushman (San) paintings.

The Amphitheatre – the most distinctive segment of the Mont-aux-Sources massif.

THE ORANGE FREE STATE

THE GOLDEN GATE

Unlike most of South Africa's other large wilderness areas, the Golden Gate Highlands National Park is more renowned for its scenic splendour than for its wildlife. It's set in the valley of the Little Caledon River, at the foot of the Maluti Mountains in the far eastern Orange Free State and is a spectacular 6 300-ha expanse of ridges and ramparts, peaks, caves, overhangs and weirdly sculpted rock formations. Seen in the slanting light of dawn and early evening, the colours of the rocks are quite remarkable, sandstone and iron oxides having combined to create a stunning array of reds, oranges, yellows and golden browns. The park takes its name from a natural 'gateway' in the form of twin, 100-m high buttresses that stand like massive sentinels and seem to glow in the sunshine.

This is a summer-rainfall area and the good rains (which average 806 mm a year) sustain a generous covering of 'sour' grasses, flowering bulbous plants and herbs and, in the damp ravines and along the streams, straggles of oldwood trees (*Leucosidea sericea*), the leaves of which were traditionally used by the Zulu to treat eye infections (the name is derived from the trees' gnarled, ancient-looking trunks).

Animals indigenous to the area include grey rhebok, the shy oribi and the mountain reedbuck. Among the game reintroduced are eland and black wildebeest, red hartebeest and plains zebra. The towering crags (the park's altitude ranges between 1 500 and 2 760 m above sea level) are home to the black eagle, jackal buzzard and bearded vulture or lammergeyer.

The 30-km, two-day Rhebok trail follows a circular route through the park, at one point cresting the 2 757-m Generaalskop, from which there are magnificent views of the 'Mountain Kingdom' of Lesotho to the south. Of the two rest-camps established in the park, Brandwag is the more sophisticated. It offers fully equipped chalets, a swimming pool, tennis courts, horses for hire, a golf course, restaurant, cocktail bar and shop.

ABOVE, AND PREVIOUS PAGE: *Iron oxides in the rock create the colour variations seen in the Golden Gate area's cliffs, peaks and buttresses.*

RIGHT: *The 90-m-high wall of the Hendrik Verwoerd dam, the country's largest reservoir.*

THE HENDRIK VERWOERD DAM

The Orange River rises in the high Maluti Mountains of Lesotho and flows for 2 250 km across the subcontinent's great central plateau, passing through the magnificent Augrabies Gorge (*see* page 69) close to the Namibian border before negotiating the final, desolate stretch to the Atlantic. It is by far South Africa's largest watercourse, draining fully 47 per cent of the country's land area.

The river's flow is erratic, dictated by seasonal rains. When the summers have been kind it becomes a fast-moving torrent that sweeps across the land in a swathe nearly 10 km wide. At other times it is benign, even modest. For almost its entire length it passes through dry, sometimes arid countryside, generally flattish, featureless and dull in colour but enlivened by skirtings of bright greenery along the riverbanks and, increasingly, by irrigated farmlands.

Many of the farms in the central and western regions are the creation of what is known as the Orange River Project, a massive water storage and distribution scheme launched in the 1960s to meet the growing needs of the cities, industry and agriculture. The scheme's more prominent components, most of which are now in place, include the 85-km Orange-Fish Tunnel (the world's largest continuous water tunnel, driven, in one of its sections, through an entire mountain range); the Van der Kloof and Fish-Sundays canals (which irrigate the orchards of the Sundays River valley in the eastern Cape); the Welbedacht barrage (from which Bloemfontein receives its water); and, most noteworthy of all, the huge P.K. le Roux and Hendrik Verwoerd dams. The latter, South Africa's biggest reservoir, has a storage capacity of some six billion litres and covers an area of 374 km². Its wall is a little over 90 m high.

The Hendrik Verwoerd dam is a popular resort area. It also has significance in terms of conservation. Around its northern shores is an 11 000-ha nature reserve; to the east is the 21 000-ha Tussen-die-Riviere game farm; and to the south, on the Cape Province side of the dam, is the 13 000-ha Oviston nature reserve.

BLOEMFONTEIN

Capital of the Orange Free State and judicial capital of South Africa, Bloemfontein began its life in 1846 as a tiny British military outpost and residency. The origin of its name remains something of a mystery: its obvious derivation is the 'flower fountain', a spring that bubbles up near the banks of the Modder River, but in fact it seems more likely that the name commemorates an ox called Bloem, owned by farmer Rudolph Brits who had settled in the area in 1840. Bloem was given to jumping fences and eventually she paid the ultimate price when she was eaten by a lion.

The classical Appeal Court building in President Brand Street. (Bloemfontein is South Africa's judicial capital; the Appelate Division the country's highest juridical authority.)

The old Presidency, home to three of the Orange Free State's republican leaders. The building now serves as a period museum and is frequently the venue for art exhibitions, musical evenings and theatrical performances.

The Fourth Raadsaal, completed in 1893 and the old Republic's last seat of government. In the foreground is Coert Steynberg's statue of General Christiaan de Wet, most renowned of the Orange Free State's military sons.

Brits is said to have called his farm after the late and much lamented animal.

Bloemfontein grew slowly but quite graciously around its distinctive flat-topped Naval Hill. In 1897 the travelling English historian James Bryce observed that 'the town is very quiet ... one of the neatest and, in a modest way, best appointed capitals in the world. Gardens are planted with trees that are now so tall as to make the whole place seem to swim in green.' Bryce's description is still apt enough, though of course Bloemfontein has grown enormously since the turn of the century. The local economy received its most powerful impetus in 1948 with the discovery and later exploitation of the giant Free State goldfields 160 km to the north, and in 1962 this was reinforced by the massive Orange River Project. The city now has a population of some 250 000, and is largely an administrative centre. Fully 40 per cent of its economically active citizens are employed in government, para-statal, social or community services.

Among Bloemfontein's early buildings, two are rather special. One is the Raadsaal or parliament of the old Orange Free State Republic, a fine and dignified edifice completed in 1889. Greek in detail and Renaissance in form, it reflects the Classical revival of the period. The other is the Anglican cathedral which is, in its present guise, the work of the renowned architect Herbert Baker. Among the other sites of note are the Old Raadsaal, a tiny but historic one-roomed structure, the impressive National Women's Memorial, created in memory of the nearly 27 000 Boer women and children who died in the infamous concentration camps of the Anglo-Boer war, the University of the Orange Free State, and the splendid modern Sand du Plessis Theatre complex, completed in 1985 at a cost of some R60 million.

SASOLBURG

The third major centre of the industrial conurbation known as the Vaal Triangle (the others are Vereeniging and Vanderbijlpark), namely Sasolburg in the far northern Orange Free State, was established just under four decades ago as the headquarters of the country's giant synthetic fuel industry. The site was carefully chosen for its proximity to three vital elements, namely the river, which supplies the nearly 40 million litres of water the conversion process uses each day, some of the southern hemisphere's largest deposits of low-grade coal, and the voracious petrol and oil markets of the Witwatersrand, 70 km to the north.

Following the international oil crisis of the mid-1970s two other huge synthetic fuel plants made their appearance on the coalfields of the eastern Transvaal. Together, the three Sasols (the name is a kind of acronym derived from the Afrikaans version of South African Coal, Oil and Gas Corporation) represent the world's first and, to date, only commercially viable oil-from-coal enterprise.

Sasolburg has grown enormously since its birth in 1954. Whereas petroleum was once its principal preoccupation, the industrial base now rests on a great many other products such as fertilizers, superphosphates, synthetic rubber, waxes, soft detergents, aerosol propellants (the subject of much debate among environmentalists), polyethylene plastics, cyanide for the gold-mining industry, phenol for use in the manufacture of nylon and a bewildering number of lesser petro-chemicals.

All of this conjures up rather a grim picture, and indeed the proliferation of chemical works does produce a great deal of flame, fume and smell. Yet Sasolburg is by no means a dark and satanic place. Quite the contrary: the town has been beautifully laid out, its neat radial streets fringed by pleasant expanses of greenery that broaden to provide children's playgrounds and traffic-free access to schools and modern shopping centres. Some charming parks have been created and fully 70 000 trees (including 14 varieties of oak) have been planted within the municipal bounds.

The sleepless giant: Sasolburg's industries work round the clock to produce oil and petro-chemicals for the insatiable Witwatersrand markets 70 km to the north.

Transvaal Cities

THE UNION
BUILDINGS

In 1908 a close union of the four British colonies that make up the present Republic of South Africa became a distinct possibility, and Pretoria was held to be the most suitable site for the new administrative capital. There was, however, no building large enough to house the offices of the proposed new administration, so the distinguished architect Herbert Baker, then practising in Johannesburg and Cape Town, was asked to submit designs for a building that would possess the 'power to give dignity and beauty to the instrument of Government and the symbol of the Union'.

Baker visualised a site comparable to those of ancient Greek cities, where the acropolis or administrative centre had been built on some prominent hill, overlooking its city and simultaneously proudly visible to its citizens. By some fortunate chance Meintjes Kop, most conspicuous of the hills close to the centre of the city, was vacant. To the east it becomes a plateau where Baker himself had designed numerous dwellings, including Government House, built in the style known as Cape Dutch Revival.

Baker's new plans called for a building far larger than any ever built in South Africa. Two identical office blocks, each with a length of around 90 m, were to be joined by a colonnaded, bow-shaped building housing committee and conference rooms and a library. Baker also planned the layout of the amphitheatre below the Union Buildings, with seats, terraces and sculptures suggesting the Greek pattern, and formal gardens near the buildings that merged with massed trees and gave way to indigenous vegetation.

When building operations ended late in 1913, among the quantities of materials used were 14 million bricks, 14 160 m^3 of sandstone, 570 m^3 of granite and 40 000 bags of cement.

Features within the grounds include the Delville Wood Memorial and Garden of Remembrance, Pretoria War Memorial and Police Memorial, as well as statues of three South African prime ministers, namely generals Louis Botha, Jan Smuts and J.B.M. Hertzog.

RIGHT: *The crescent-shaped elegance of the Union Buildings, overlooking Pretoria from the slopes of Meintjes Kop.*

PREVIOUS PAGE: *A panoramic view of Pretoria – also known as the Jacaranda City – with the Union Buildings visible in the background.*

CHURCH SQUARE

At the heart of Pretoria's city centre, is Church Square. About 6 ha in size, this was the original market square where ox-wagons were outspanned while their owners went about their business at the row of little shops that once fronted onto it. The little church that gave it its name no longer stands, but there is still much that speaks of the old Zuid-Afrikaansche Republiek (Transvaal Republic).

At the centre the statue of President Paul Kruger – guarded by the bronze figures of four burghers – faces north towards the Palace of Justice. This is statuary with a story, starting in 1895 when an amiable millionaire, Sammy Marks, donated money to the city of Pretoria for a statue of the president. It was executed by sculptor Anton van Wouw, cast in bronze in Italy and then shipped back to the republic via Maputo (then Lourenço Marques). Unfortunately, the Anglo-Boer War of 1899-1902 had just broken out, so the statue stayed in storage at the harbour until 1912.

The following year it was unveiled in Prince's Park, Pretoria West, but without the four supporting figures, which had meanwhile disappeared. When the four supporters were traced in England, the completed group was moved to the front of the railway station. However, having been designed originally for Church Square, it was finally moved to its present site in 1954.

The old Raadsaal, or council chamber of Kruger's republic, was completed in 1890, and the ornately fronted Palace of Justice was completed in 1899. Like the Raadsaal, it has a frontage divided into five sections, and the two buildings complement one another well as they look down with tolerance on the bands of citizens who gather ocasionally in praise or protest.

The Palace of Justice provides a stately background for Anton van Wouw's bronze statute of 'Oom Paul' Kruger, president of the South African Republic (the Transvaal) from 1883 until his flight into exile in 1900.

PRETORIA CENTRAL

With a length of some 26 km, Church Street may well be the longest straight city street in the world, as some Pretorians claim. In springtime, with other streets of the capital, it forms a tunnel of hazy mauve or purple as countless jacaranda trees blossom to greet the warming spring sun. It's forgotten now that Pretoria was once known as 'the city of roses' – the jacarandas, brought originally from Brazil, have been planted since 1888 and today they bedeck hundreds of kilometres of streets and most of Pretoria's approximately 100 public parks and gardens.

On Church Street is the Kruger House Museum in what once was the home of the old president, who enjoyed sitting on its shady stoep to exchange pleasantries with passers-by or dispense homespun wisdom over endless cups of coffee. The lions on the gateposts, so at odds with the unpretentiousness of the house, were the gift of a grateful industrialist who had received a presidential favour. Just across the road, and also bereft of adornment, is the church at which Kruger was a regular attendant.

History was also made – and indeed signed – in the much grander chambers of Melrose House, built in 1886 for George Heys, the wealthy owner of a stagecoach line. Here Boer and British delegations met on the evening of 31 May 1902 to sign the Treaty of Vereeniging that ended the Anglo-Boer War.

A grandson of Queen Victoria lies buried in Pretoria. Prince Christian Victor died of fever while serving with the British Army in 1900, and Prince's Park is a reminder of this historical footnote. Just across Church Street from the park is Heroes' Acre, where many republican stalwarts lie buried, as well as prominent figures from more recent history. Pretoria's oldest suburb is Arcadia, followed by Sunnyside, and both were incorporated into the city around 1890. For many years the only means of crossing the Apies River to get to Arcadia was by the old Lion Bridge which, after more than a century, still faithfully carries Church Street across the now canalised waters.

ABOVE: *The official reception room of Paul Kruger's home, presented to the aging patriarch in 1883. The modest house has been faithfully restored to its original character; on view are Kruger's furniture and personal belongings and, behind the building, his carriage and a stinkwood trek-wagon.*

Melrose House, the 19th-century mansion in which, on 31 May 1902, the Peace Treaty of Vereeniging was signed, bringing to an end the protracted and bitterly fought Anglo-Boer War.

Jacarandas in their November glory. The first two saplings, costing £10 apiece, were imported from Rio de Janeiro in 1888; today some 70 000 of these feathery, lilac-flowered trees decorate the city.

One of the striking pieces of ornamentation that decorate Pretoria's State Theatre complex in Church Street, home of the various companies of the Performing Arts Council of the Transvaal.

Pretoria Art Museum, repository of works by such South African artists as Pierneef, Van Wouw and Frans Oerder, and for part of the Lady Michaelis collection of Dutch and Flemish paintings.

PRETORIA MUSEUMS

There is a strong case for believing that some of the final stages in the evolution of man took place on the southern African veld, and the Transvaal's major archaeological sites of Kromdraai, Swartkrans and Makapansgat are world famous. The Transvaal Museum of Natural History in Paul Kruger Street brings under one roof artefacts from these sites and others, and combines them with displays of reptiles, amphibians and insects under the theme of Life's Genesis. In addition the museum incorporates the Austin Roberts Bird Hall and the museum of the Geological Survey, which displays the country's earliest known gold crusher, a rounded boulder to which a plank was attached in such a manner that the boulder could be rocked like a see-saw.

Technology of a somewhat more up-to-date nature can be found in the South African Museum of Science and Technology, where atoms and nuclear energy, space travel and the wonders of water are among the subjects displayed. The Post Office Museum shows the steady advance of particular fields of technology, from morse to microwaves and beyond, with a fascinating re-creation of an old-time post office, complete with all its antique and ornate equipment. The National Cultural History and Open-Air Museum is another repository of relics of the old South African Republic, from coins to costumes, firearms to furniture, and much else besides.

Military history is the theme of two museums appropriately housed in two forts that were built just before the end of the 19th century and since then restored. There were four forts originally, designed and sited principally to protect the capital against attack or invasion by the troublesome 'uitlanders' or foreigners who, while making a good living from the Witwatersrand's gold, had little sympathy for the country's ultra-conservative government. The displays in Fort Schanskop cover the period from the era of the muzzle-loader to the Anglo-Boer War of 1899-1902, while those at Fort Klapperkop depict aspects of the World Wars, South African involvement in the Korean War and the protracted 'border war' of more recent times.

Part of the 'Life's Genesis' exhibition at the Transvaal Museum of Natural History. The bronze bust is that of archaeologist Robert Broom, who is noted for his research into Australopithecine man.

THE VOORTREKKER MONUMENT

The Great Trek was an attempt by Afrikaner farmers to evade what they considered to be the unjust and unduly liberal British administration of the Cape of Good Hope in the 1830s. Officially condemned at the time by their own Dutch Reformed Church, the movement was later to be vested with deep spiritual significance, leading to a resurgence of pride in Afrikaner history and identity. This occurred in 1938, the year regarded as the centenary of the trek. The principal focus of celebrations commemorating those events was a symbolic trek of 12 wagons drawn by oxen that converged on Pretoria from various points about the country.

The official date of their arrival was 16 December, itself of significance as the centenary of the date on which a Voortrekker commando defeated a Zulu army at Blood River in Natal. At Monument Hill in Pretoria and at Blood River, cornerstones for monuments were laid. The design of the Voortrekker Monument is that of architect Gerard Moerdijk (1890-1958). The central building stands 40 m high, on a base 40 m square, and is entered after climbing 70 steps, while a further 260 steps inside lead to a vaulted dome from which there is an impressive view. At precisely noon on 16 December, a ray of sunlight shines through an aperture in the dome to light the words 'Ons vir jou, Suid Afrika' on a cenotaph far below in the Hall of Heroes.

The building is of granite and is surrounded by a symbolic laager of 64 stone ox-wagons. It was officially opened on 16 December 1949 before a crowd estimated at 250 000, or some 17 per cent of the total Afrikaner population at the time.

In painting, tapestry and carved marble murals the story of the trek and of specific incidents is graphically told. Adjoining the monument is a museum in which many original Voortrekker items are displayed. Open-air religious services and other meetings are often held in the large amphitheatre surrounding the monument.

ABOVE: *The monolithic Voortrekker Monument: a memorial to the republican founders, and a symbol of Afrikaner national identity.*

THE UNIVERSITY OF SOUTH AFRICA

At night, row upon row of lighted windows and the stark, back-lit outline can create the impression of some gigantic ocean liner strangely transported far inland, and in daylight this vast complex is seen to have been built in assertively modern style. These are the main buildings of the University of South Africa (widely known as Unisa), inaugurated in 1973 on Muckleneuk Ridge in the southern part of Pretoria and believed to be the first university in the world to teach entirely by correspondence.

Unisa had its origins exactly a century earlier, in 1873, as the University of the Cape of Good Hope. University education, and even education at secondary level, developed relatively late in South Africa: among the first secondary schools was the South African College, founded in 1829, which developed into the University of Cape Town

(although a school of the same name still exists). The 1850s saw the establishment of colleges, later to become universities, in Bloemfontein and Grahamstown, and in 1866 the University of Stellenbosch had its beginnings as the Stellenbosch gymnasium. But the University of South Africa is the direct descendant of the first southern African university.

Established by royal charter under the seal of Queen Victoria, the University of the Cape of Good Hope, at Cape Town, was empowered to set examinations and to award degrees, though without taking any part in teaching. In 1916, when it became the federal University of South Africa, incorporating six university colleges in all four provinces of the then Union of South Africa, the university moved its headquarters to Pretoria. The establishment of its Division of External Studies in 1946 developed study by correspondence and led to its reconstitution as an 'external' university in 1951.

Growth has been rapid, and by 1990 Unisa had departments of Arts, Economics, Science, Education, Law and Theology, with an enrolment of 104 302 students, of whom 12 093 resided outside South Africa.

ABOVE: *Unisa, largest of South Africa's institutions of higher learning and one of the largest correspondence universities in the world.*

Pretoria Zoo ranks among the world's biggest and best: it is home to some 3 500 southern African and exotic wildlife species, including the four great apes, a host of mammals and birds (pictured here are pink flamingoes), the rare South American maned wolf and the only known giant eland in captivity.

THE NATIONAL ZOOLOGICAL GARDENS

Pretoria Zoo, as it is popularly known, is the oldest zoological gardens in South Africa, having been founded in 1899 on the site it still occupies, now enlarged to some 55 ha among the city's northern suburbs. From its source in Fountains Valley, the Apies River, named after the engaging little vervet monkey, flows through the zoo with its backdrop of massive stone terraces and cable-cars that transport visitors to strategic view sites.

Most of the animals here (there are some 140 mammal species) are not indigenous to southern Africa but come from many parts of the continent and, indeed, from other continents. Many species threatened with extinction have been bred here, including the pygmy hippopotamus, American bison and orang-utan, and it was here that the first white rhinoceros was born in captivity. A special feature is the antelope collection which also contains species that are rare and endangered in the wild. Among them are the giant eland, the oryx, and the spiral-horned addax from the desert regions of north Africa. A breeding herd of each species has been established.

In addition to the larger animals, there are about 200 bird species, and a reptile collection that includes fully grown and fearsome crocodiles, iguanas and cold-eyed snakes. Altogether more amiable is the aquarium, with its sections for freshwater and seawater creatures, and a vast collection of shells from many shores. Although display is an important and obvious function of the zoo, great emphasis is placed on conservation, and courses are offered on such subjects as ecology and bird identification.

One of the most captivating exhibits is not zoological at all. This is the huge cast-iron confection known as the Sammy Marks' Fountain, complete with pillars, cupola and pensive classical figures. A gift to the city from the wealthy industrialist, it was shipped from Scotland in pieces and assembled on Church Square, where it stood for many years before being displaced by the statue of Paul Kruger (*see* page 118).

DOORNKLOOF

Doornkloof, the family home of Jan Christiaan Smuts, who was arguably the 20th century's greatest South African. This modest house has been restored to its original condition and now serves as a museum in which Smuts's simple furniture, and various memorabilia, are displayed.

That intensely complex and brilliant South African statesman known to the world as General Smuts (although he held the higher rank of Field Marshal in the British army) came from simple and humble beginnings, and liked to be at home among unpretentious surroundings at Doornkloof near the village of Irene.

Born at Riebeeck West in the Western Cape in 1870, Jan Christiaan Smuts only went to the local village school at the age of 12 years, but matriculated with distinction just five years later at Victoria College, now the University of Stellenbosch. Further academic laurels were gathered at Cape Town and Cambridge University, where he read law. Turbulent events in South Africa saw him shift allegiance from Cecil Rhodes to Kruger's Transvaal, where he became State Attorney at the age of 28. In the Anglo-Boer War of 1899-1902 Smuts put aside high office and rode off to do battle, rising to the rank of general. He was still active in the field at the very end.

It was in 1909 that he bought a small farm near Irene, 16 km from Pretoria. There was no house on it, so he looked for something inexpensive to put up, something temporary that could be replaced by a better and more permanent dwelling once the farm started to pay. He bought a timber-framed building of corrugated iron that had served as a mess for British officers during the war, and transported it sheet by sheet to the site where it stands today. The 'better' house was never built. As a need arose for more space, so another room was added, and another. And even though Jan Smuts eventually strode the world stage, this rambling house was always home. When the British royal family visited South Africa in 1947, Smuts did not hesitate to entertain them at Doornkloof.

JOHANNESBURG

Literally built on gold, Johannesburg may be said to have had its birth on a Sunday in February 1886 when an outcrop of the Main Reef was discovered more or less by accident. The site where George Harrison pegged his discoverer's claim, sold it soon after for a paltry sum and then walked away, perhaps to seek an easier fortune, is still preserved in the park that bears his name. Certainly he could not have known that he was turning his back on the greatest goldfield in the world.

There is some dispute as to which Johannes the city's name commemorates, but there can be no mistaking the identity of Johannesburg itself. It is a city on the go, with a central business district of uncompromising modernity, yet with tranquil, green spaces such as Joubert Park, laid out as

The city-centre skyline of Johannesburg, South Africa's financial capital and largest city. In the foreground is Village Main gold mine, now a recycling unit, extracting gold from old mine dumps.

long ago as 1887 and still preserved as a calm oasis among the glass and concrete edifices that rise from the hot asphalt.

A number of the city's parks are traversed by the Braam-fontein Spruit Trail, a hiking way that combines history with lakes, bird sanctuaries and even the Johannesburg Botanic Garden on the shores of Emmarentia Dam.

Johannesburg is a rapidly growing city, its profile changing almost by the month. One of the more recent additions is the concrete-and-glass Times Media building in Diagonal Street.

The Market Theatre, an 80-year-old building that once did duty as the Indian fruit and citrus market, houses four auditoria, a shopping arcade and restaurants, including a bistro noted for its unusual 'Klippies' jazz bar. A 400-stall flea market is held on the adjacent Mary Fitzgerald Square each Saturday.

A favourite space is the Zoo (the Johannesburg Zoological Gardens) in Hermann Eckstein Park, with its cleverly sculptured enclosures for hundreds of species of mammals, birds and reptiles. Zoo Lake is the venue for unhurried boating, and its banks offer shade for picnics, while near at hand is the most visited of all Johannesburg's many museums, the South African National Museum of Military History. Although the city boasts of its modernity, there are always times and places for gentler pursuits than business.

Above all, perhaps, Johannesburg is its people, a rich and varied mix drawn from all over the world, many forming associations aimed at maintaining national contacts and preserving old traditions. Like the most mixed and most densely populated high-rise suburb of Hillbrow, which is said never to sleep, Johannesburg itself also creates the impression that at all times there is something happening.

IMPERIAL
ARCHITECTURE

The mining pioneers on the Rand lived in tents, wagons, or any sort of shelter they could throw together. However, the demands of deep-level mining soon attracted corporate capital and, as fortunes were made the haphazard settlements gave way to handsome streets lined with tall, brick houses. In 1892 a young architect named Herbert Baker arrived at the Cape, where he popularised the style known as Cape Dutch Revival before, inevitably, being drawn to the Transvaal. Here, in addition to several public and state buildings, he designed over 300 houses, many of them 'mansions for the magnates'. One such house was the opulent and immense Northwards, built in 1904 for Col. John Dale Lace. The Cape gables have become elongated and somewhat Flemish in appearance, but the interior fittings faithfully reflect the best of the old Cape, with

The Rand Regiments' War Memorial, designed by the celebrated British architect Sir Edwin Lutyens and erected in a patch of woodland near the Zoo, commemorates men of the Witwatersrand killed during the Anglo-Boer War (1899-1902).

beamed ceilings and glazed wall-cupboards with gently gabled tops.

When no suitable designs from local architects were submitted for the proposed Johannesburg Art Gallery, Baker wholeheartedly supported the commissioning of the well-known British architect Edwin Lutyens who had already agreed to design the Rand Regiments' War Memorial.

Massive in stone, and surmounted by a 4,8 m sphere and figure by the French sculptor Aronson, the memorial is a dignified and impressive reminder of the men of the Rand

regiments who died in the war of 1899-1902. The art gallery reflects Lutyens' return to the Classical style, with its imposing porticoed facade and interior of perfectly proportioned interleading halls. Unfortunately, lack of funds prevented the gallery from being completed, though some additions were carried out in the 1930s. Then, in 1986, a new section was added. Designed by local architects and built in the post-modern idiom, it skilfully complements the classical lines of the original.

Baker left South Africa in 1912, and although he left behind a great many buildings to perpetuate his memory, his moments of greatest prestige still lay ahead. Together with Lutyens he went on to design the architectural jewel in the great British imperial crown – the administrative centre of New Delhi in India.

'Northwards', designed by Sir Herbert Baker in the manner of the Arts and Crafts Movement, was completed in 1904. Its frontage is distinguished by rough stone walls, gables and a magnificent oriel window.

The total compatibility of the newly designed section of the Johannesburg Art Gallery with the Lutyens designed rooms beyond is clearly evident in this picture, which has also captured two paintings by the eminent South African painter Hendrik Pierneef (1886-1957).

ELLIS PARK

Given that its people have a reputation for being 'sport crazy', it is not surprising that South Africa has numerous first-class sporting venues. Named after a former mayor of Johannesburg, the original Ellis Park was laid out on the site of a brickfield near the old Waterworks Dam in the lower part of New Doornfontein. Before this, the original sports ground was the Wanderers, a club ground where the first rugby test match to take place in the Transvaal was played as long ago as 1896.

The foundations of both rugby and cricket in the Transvaal were well and truly laid at the old Wanderers, the Transvaal Rugby Union moving to Ellis Park only in 1928. Money for the development of the new ground was derived in large measure from the sale of a site which had been set aside for a dog-racing track. Dog-racing, however, was subsequently prohibited by law, and rugby has thrived there ever since, year after year thrilling crowds with nail-biting play between Springboks and numerous international teams, as well as inter-provincial contests for the coveted Currie and Lion Cups.

In recent years, however, soccer has become a serious rival for first place in the hearts of South African sports addicts, and standards have dramatically risen since 1950 when one of South Africa's few soccer internationals – against an Australian team – was played on the rugby field at Ellis Park. In fact, before the construction of Soccer City on the outskirts of Soweto, Ellis Park was a favourite venue for the game.

But Ellis Park is more than rugby – or even soccer. It provides seating for 5 000 spectators at its tennis stadium, and for 8 000 more at its indoor tennis arena. There is also an Olympic-standard swimming pool within the grounds, helping to make the place a truly all-round venue for sportslovers.

The 100 000-capacity Ellis Park stadium, venue of rugby matches and championship soccer.

THE MINES

Johannesburg's typical mine dumps, now receiving attention from horticulturists, are silent evidence of the underground activity that never ceases. Towering headgear structures, some stark and silent, others endlessly raising and lowering men, machines and gold, confirm the reason for Johannesburg's existence.

There had been gold strikes before the riches of the Witwatersrand were discovered; for example, those in the low-lying eastern Transvaal where men toiled and, almost inevitably it seemed, died of fever. Fairly soon, however, the easily won alluvial gold was worked out and the happy-

Headgear and mine dumps are synonymous with the Witwatersrand. This is one of the less sightly dumps; many others wear thin coats of greenery.

go-lucky survivors of that gold rush moved on to the next. In the case of the Witwatersrand, however, as the reef dipped ever further underground, the era of small-time prospecting came to an end. In its place came money, machines and labour on an unprecedented scale – the only way to unlock the vast subterranean treasure chest.

Among the first lodes to be exploited was the Crown Reef, where the company called Crown Mines Limited was for many years the largest single producer of gold in the world. Today the old mine is a tourist attraction at the heart of Gold Reef City, a reconstruction of early Johannesburg. Here visitors can enter the cage at the head of the shaft and be whisked underground to inspect the workings of a real gold mine. On street level, shops, businesses, and places of entertainment and refreshment provide a very real feeling of history. There is even a Victorian fun-fair. And for those who want to prolong the experience, the 'city's' hotel provides four-star accommodation – with a few concessions to the present.

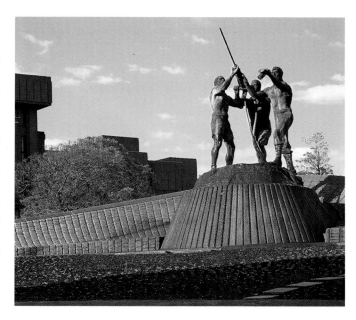

TOP: *The powerful monument to the miners who created Johannesburg, and who have sustained the city over the past century, can be seen below the Civic Centre in Braamfontein.*

ABOVE: *The old ten-stamp battery at George Harrison Park at Langlaagte, site of the very first claims pegged and registered. Harrison is said to have sold his share for just £10.*

LEFT: *Gold Reef City on the Crown Mines site is an imaginative reconstruction of early Johannesburg. Among its attractions are the old underground workings, steam train and horse-drawn omnibus trips, a Victorian fun-fair, a replica of the Theatre Royale, speciality shops, and many individual re-creations – of an early brewery, a Chinese laundry, a cooperage, a newspaper office and the stock exchange.*

ABOVE: *Visitors to Gold Reef City are able to watch the metal being poured. Crown Mines' No 14 shaft, centrepiece of the 'living museum', yielded an impressive 1,4 million kg of gold during its lifetime. At one time the mine also held the world shaft-sinking record.*

RIGHT: *Urban monotony. The more affluent Sowetans – the growing number of entrepreneurs, professional people and highly qualified executives – have substantial and attractive homes. But most residents live in grossly overcrowded conditions. Pictured is one of the newer housing developments.*

SOWETO

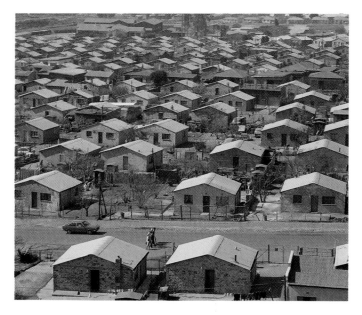

To some, Soweto is Africa rising, to others it is Africa descending. Soweto is indeed these contrasts, but also many things between. The name is derived from South Western Townships, and the place is a large, albeit unproclaimed, city formed by the loose amalgamation of several smaller settlements that sprang up on farms within the municipal area of greater Johannesburg.

The rambling patchwork of roads and dwellings, which range from the immaculate to the 'informal', is home to more than one million people, most of whom find employment in the adjoining city of Johannesburg. Soweto has a growing affluent class whose members include professionals and executives who live in large and luxurious homes, but home for most Sowetans is considerably less grand. The provision of infrastructure, such as the reticulation of water and electricity, is fairly advanced, and many clinics, hospitals and schools have been built. To these facilities was recently added one of the four campuses of the new Vista University.

Largely unencumbered by the restrictions of officialdom, trade and commerce flourish, and artisans, many of them untrained, show an enviable skill and ingenuity in maintaining and repairing a variety of complex goods, from electrical appliances to motor vehicles. Well over 2 000 shops supply the diverse wants of Sowetans, cash or barter being acceptable forms of trade in many of them.

Relaxation for many people is to be found in one of the large number of shebeens – increasingly sophisticated places for drinking and for social contact. Community halls and other places of entertainment have bred a vibrant musical culture – mbaqanga – that is essentially 'township'. By far the most popular sport, with important matches attended by tens of thousands of highly partisan spectators, is soccer. Outside the stadia and fields, it is rare to find a corner where small boys, the stars of tomorrow, are not enthusiastically kicking a ball.

Soweto at sunset, with coal fires burning. The country's largest 'black' township (though the collapse of the apartheid system has made the term obsolete) sprawls over 95 km² to the south-west of Johannesburg. It is home to about two million people.

THE NORTHERN & EASTERN
TRANSVAAL

THE MAGALIESBERG

The ridge that runs due westwards from a point near Pretoria to the Rustenburg area 120 km away is by no definition a major range of hills (it rises a modest 300 m above the surrounding, rather flattish countryside), but it has a special charm of its own. Beneath the hills the land lies at a lower altitude than that of the classic Highveld to the east, and the climate is kind, the rains generally good and the air in the parklike valleys of the Hex, Sterkstroom and Magalies rivers limpid and warm, even on winter days. The warmth and water sustain the region's marvellously rich harvests of subtropical fruits, peaches, oranges, tobacco, vegetables and flowers.

Predictably, the Magaliesberg is a popular weekend and holiday destination for people who live in the concrete labyrinths of the Witwatersrand, just an hour's drive away. Some come for its convenient position, half-way between

PREVIOUS PAGE: *The Hartebeespoort Dam from the pleasant slopes of the Magaliesberg.*

Hartebeespoort Dam, and its nature reserve below the Magaliesberg range, ranks as one of the Transvaal's most popular weekend recreation areas.

the Pretoria-Johannesburg conurbation and the glittering playground of Sun City to the north (*see* pages 146-7), but most are attracted by the 1620-ha Hartbeespoort Dam (which functions both as a source of irrigation and as a popular resort area), the tranquillity of the hills and valleys, the scenic drives, challenging hikes and gentle rambles that the region offers.

The hills are among the last refuges of the shy and stately Cape Vulture, a species that depends for survival on bones of carcasses crushed to digestible size by the powerful jaws of the hyaena, a scavenger that has all but disappeared from the region. On the endangered list, the birds are sustained by the 'vulture restaurants' that have been established and, in the breeding season, by their forays onto the game-rich plains of the relatively new Pilanesberg National Park to the north.

NDEBELE VILLAGE

The Ndebele are among the longest-established recent immigrants to the Transvaal – some of the ancestors of these Nguni people are thought to have arrived from Natal before the year 1650. Tradition has it that the Ndebele of the south-eastern areas are descended from an ancestor called Musi, who came from 'the land of the Zulu'. Those of the northern Transvaal are descended from chief Langalibalele, who once ruled in the area that is now Durban.

The southern Ndebele, especially, are noted for the artistic decorations they apply to their clothing and the walls of their homes. The traditional dwelling unit was used almost exclusively as a sleeping place, and the various units of a village were linked by walls of clay. Each home was originally a circular wall topped by a pointed roof of thatching reed, the classic 'cone-on-cylinder' configuration. In more recent times, however, rectangular dwellings with flat roofs have been built, the additional

ABOVE: *Bright geometrical patterns decorate this typical Ndebele home in a showpiece village near Marula, Bophuthatswana.*

wall area providing the Ndebele artists – usually the womenfolk – with a larger canvas on which to execute the stylised decorations.

These take the form of triangles, rectangles and other basic shapes, originally painted in white, grey and brownish shades of natural ochre. Soot was mixed with clay to deepen the shades, all the way to black, and many an artist-housewife favoured the softer tones derived from the addition of a cake or two of washing-blue or indigo. In addition to basic designs and wall panels based on their own intricate and colourful beadwork, Ndebele murals may show scenes of modern cities with many features of current urban life. Apart from paintings, buildings are enriched by delicate, decorative architectural touches, usually in moulded clay, such as pediments, turrets and finials.

Ndebele clothing is colourful, too, adult women wearing an apron of beaded oxhide with, traditionally, a black back panel. For weddings and other ceremonial occasions, an apron of more elaborate design is worn, with five heavily beaded flaps. The tribal blanket, often attractively ornamented with beads, is the usual outer garment, and has stripes of purple, yellow, blue, green and red. Heads are sometimes shaven, leaving tufts of hair from which small ornaments may be hung. Bands of plaited grass, covered with beadwork in red, blue and white, are worn around the neck, limbs and waist, while married women wear rings of brass, often piled one upon the other.

SUN CITY

One of the world's best-known hotel-casino resorts, Sun City in the quasi-independent republic of Bophuthatswana north-west of Johannesburg, is an enormous glittering extravaganza dedicated to entertaining, amusing and pampering holidaymakers in their hedonistic thousands.

There are three hotels on the site, ranging from the informal, family-orientated Cabanas through to the luxurious Sun City Hotel (distinguished by its foyer, a mirrored, Tivoli-lighted cavern the size of a soccer pitch) to the even more plush Cascades, a 15-storey, twin-pyramid building. The grounds of the latter are both extensive and beautiful, as over 50 km^2 of the surrounding countryside have been landscaped to produce a fantasia of lawns, pools, grottos, waterfalls, tropical plants and exotic bird life. A fourth hotel, the grandest of all, is planned. This will be called the Palace, and will be an elaborate 350-room affair of domes and minarets vaguely reminiscent of the Raj at its most

OPPOSITE: *The Sun City complex comprises three hotels (a fourth is being developed), a casino and entertainment centre and a vast array of sporting and recreation facilities.*

BELOW: *The plush, twin-pyramid Cascades hotel offers the ultimate in luxury. Together with its magnificent grounds it is a leisure-seeker's paradise.*

opulent. The grounds (ten times the size of those surrounding the Cascades) will feature a 'jungle' of 3 500 trees and a vast swimming pool in which two-metre-high surfing waves will be artificially created.

Of Sun City's many other components, perhaps the most notable are the casino (which offers the full range of gaming tables together with about a thousand one-armed bandits); Waterworld, a 750-m-long man-made recreation lake; the Gary Player Country Club and its splendid golf course (on which many of the world's greats have played and which hosts the annual Million Dollar Golf Challenge); and the Entertainment Centre. This last is a vibrant concentration of restaurants and bars, nightclubs, discos and cinemas, a computerized bingo hall, a 620-seat Extravaganza Theatre, and – the focal point – the Superbowl, used for lavish promotions, conventions, world title fights, big-name shows and banquets for up to 1 300 guests at one sitting.

Sun City is set, incongruously perhaps, in one of the bleaker, less developed parts of the subcontinent. But for all the contrast, the splendour among relative poverty, the place has proved a blessing to the region since it first opened its doors in 1979, as it provides work for more than 3 000 people, most of them local Tswana. For every person on its staff there are five others who gain indirect employment, and a lot of the money generated by the resort goes towards the provision of schools, clinics, houses and much-needed services.

THE PANORAMA ROUTE

This is a world of climbers, views, and eagles – misty vistas of fields and forests stretching far to the sunrise over Africa. Overlooking it all, an easy, lazy loop of road hugs the edge of the escarpment, where the northern Drakensberg falls away sheer to the Lowveld. This is one end of a drive that is named – with every justification – the Panorama Route. This, in turn, is part of a more extensive scenic excursion called the Summit Route.

The start may be said to be the Long Tom Pass, a route known to the old-time wagoners as the 'harbour road' because it eventually led to the port at Delagoa Bay. Today sinuous coils of roadway embrace the foothills where retreating Boer fighters dragged two of their great Schneider siege-guns out of reach of the British army in 1900. A full-scale replica of one of the guns that both Boer and Brit called the Long Tom stands close to the road in a lonely, lovely setting.

Tumbling rivers once flashed with the yellow gleam of gold, and treasure-seekers from all over the world made the pilgrimage to this corner of the Transvaal. Gravel from the deep pools below the falls called Mac-Mac, Bridal Veil, Panorama, Lisbon and Berlin was panned for gold and success was commemorated in the name of Bourke's Luck, where river-borne stones have eroded the rock to form a spectacular system of pot-holes.

Just below Bourke's Luck, the combined streams of the Blyde and Treur rivers (the rivers of joy and of sorrow, respectively) have carved a deep canyon stretching some 26 km along the line of the escarpment, eventually reaching the Lowveld. Dammed in the upper reaches of the canyon, the river forms the central feature of a vast nature reserve, with holiday resorts and camp-sites within a short hike of rich indigenous flora. Large antelope have been re-introduced to the area which is traversed by the Blyde River Canyon Hiking Trail that starts at the well-named feature of God's Window.

The Blyde River Canyon, one of the great natural wonders of Africa. Towering almost a kilometre above the red sandstone gorge are the massive cliffs of the Three Rondavels.

Superb viewsites along much of the Panorama Route enable travellers to gaze across the immensity of the Lowveld plain to the west. Pictured here is the view from God's Window.

*The delicate twin cascade of the Lisbon Falls near the escarpment
village of Graskop. The area is famed for the number and variety of
its waterfalls; among especially lovely ones are the Bridal Veil, the
Mac-Mac, the Berlin, the Horsehoe and the Lone Creek.*

PILGRIM'S REST

The pilgrims of this town's name were those adventurers who, if they didn't rest here where a stream flowed to the Blyde River, pitched their tents and energetically panned for gold. The great gold rush occurred in 1874, and exceptionally large nuggets were found in the area, including one that weighed almost 8 kg.

The atmosphere of those heady days is successfully evoked by the restoration of the old village, where most settlers built dwellings of corrugated iron because they weren't sure how long the conservative Transvaal government would tolerate their presence. If turned out, they reasoned, they could at least carry their houses with them. Besides, they expected the gold to be exhausted within a year or two anyway. The alluvial gold did give out fairly soon, but mining operations continued until 1971, when the entire village was purchased by the Transvaal Provincial Administration for the establishment of an open-air, working museum.

For those who are curious about the lifestyle of the early gold-seekers, there are daily demonstrations of panning for gold along the banks of the Pilgrim's Creek. The Royal Hotel, of which the bar was once a convent chapel in Lourenço Marques (now Maputo), again receives guests in restored premises and annexes. The comforts of 'home' and the differences between an ordinary miner and a mine manager are well illustrated in the stark simplicity of the miner's house museum contrasted to Art Deco Alanglade, the manager's mansion discreetly out of sight of the village. Pilgrim's Rest not only offers a fascinating glimpse into history, but is well sited as a base to explore the attractions of the Summit Route.

The main street of Pilgrim's Rest – a prosperous little forestry village of some 400 residents, it is also a 'living museum'. The buildings, dating from the area's golden age – the period 1880-1915 – have been faithfully restored to their original condition.

SUDWALA

Situated within a hill known as Mankelekele, or 'crag upon crag', the Sudwala caves were formed by the steady seepage of water along fault lines in dolomitic limestone. These were gradually eroded into the large caverns

One of Sudwala's many strangely-shaped dripstone formations. Most impressive of the chambers is the P.A. Owen Hall, a natural theatre complete with 'stalls', 'gallery' and perfect acoustics.

and passages, still not completely explored, that make up these caves. Further percolation of surface water slowly created the many dripstone formations which may grow by as little as one-tenth of a millimetre in a year, depending on conditions such as wind and humidity. The cave system is kept naturally at a constant average temperature of 20°C, but the source of the unfailing stream of fresh air still awaits discovery. (The sections of caves open to tourists comprise only a tiny proportion of the full length of this incredible natural wonder. Local legend maintains that the end is several kilometres away, deep in the dolomitic mass.)

Prehistoric man discovered the caves but they are named after a Swazi nobleman, Sudwala, who took refuge here during a period of inter-tribal upheaval early in the 19th century. Attempts to smoke him out by lighting a huge fire at the cave mouth were unsuccessful, but are said to have left the stains still visible on the rock.

The immense size of some of the formations, such as the fancifully named Screaming Monster or the 14-m Rocket Silo, indicates a very great age indeed. This is confirmed by the fossilized remains, visible on the roof, of colonies of primitive algae called stromatolites which have been dated to around 2 000 million years before the present – these are one of the very earliest recognised life forms on earth.

The P.R. Owen Hall is a natural dome-roofed amphitheatre within the cave system. The gently raked floor and excellent acoustics are as nature created them, and the 'hall' makes an unusual and satisfactory venue for musical recitals.

Dinosaurs stalk a hillside close to the cave entrance amid a setting of indigenous vegetation including cycads, those palm-like descendants of primitive flora. The dinosaurs are fearsomely accurate reconstructions, to full scale, of such creatures as the flesh-devouring *Tyrannosaurus rex* and the heavily armoured *Triceratops.* Busts of various forms of early man look on, though separated in time from the great age of reptiles by many millions of years.

Near the entrance to the caves is the Dinosaur Park, a fascinating open-air display featuring life-size replicas of the giant reptiles that ruled the earth some 250 million years ago.

THE KRUGER NATIONAL PARK

For all the ease and comfort with which the tourist is surrounded, this most famous of game reserves nevertheless presents old Africa untamed. Here are lion and leopard, lordly elephant, hippo and rhino, herds of buffalo, kudu and sable, all living and interacting in a wilderness unchanged over thousands of years.

The park is named after Paul Kruger, the stern old president of the old Transvaal Republic. About 18 months before the outbreak of the Anglo-Boer War (1899-1902) it was he who caused the first conservation area, the Sabie game reserve, to be proclaimed. After the war, a former major of dragoons, James Stevenson-Hamilton, was appointed the reserve's first game warden. In 1946 he retired as chief warden, laden with honours and counting among his accomplishments a hand in the establishment of the National Parks Board. Skukuza, the 'capital' of the park, is named in his honour, this being the name given to him by the local tribespeople who likened his clearing out of poachers to the actions of a man of great thoroughness, 'he who scrapes clean'. His untiring efforts laid the foundations for the magnificent wildlife reserve of today.

The extent of the park is close to 20 000 km^2, a Lowveld paradise of savanna grassland and bush. Many areas, especially those near permanent water, are characterized by a great variety of tree forms. The natural boundaries of the park are the Crocodile River in the south, the Limpopo in the north and the Lebombo Mountains of the Mozambique border in the east. The western boundary, through which most visitors enter the park, is marked by fences that are inconspicuous amid the bush.

Within these bounds the park is home to an impressive number of denizens of the wild: 137 mammal species and 114 reptile, 33 amphibian, 450 bird, 227 butterfly and 40 fish species. In the Kruger National Park, there is always something to surprise the visitor, as well as to delight and to teach.

BELOW: *Giant and ancient baobab trees are a common sight in the park. Some specimens live for more than 1 000 years, their branches achieving a spread of nearly 40 m.*

ABOVE: *The Kruger's rest-camps are carefully sited to take advantage of natural attractions – some overlook river or waterhole, others afford fine views of the Lowveld countryside.*

LEFT: *Hippo and elephant drink together at one of the park's perennial rivers. The Kruger's elephant population numbers about 8 000; other large mammals include both black and white rhino, lion, leopard, cheetah, buffalo and giraffe.*

THE CAPE PENINSULA
1. Table Mountain
2. Historic Cape Town
3. City Squares
4. The Company's Garden
5. Cape Town Harbour
6. The Nico Malan Theatre Complex
7. The Atlantic Seaboard
8. False Bay
9. Groot Constantia
10. Kirstenbosch
11. Groote Schuur Estate

THE WESTERN CAPE
12. Franschhoek
13. Paarl
14. Stellenbosch
15. Tulbagh
16. The Overberg
17. Swellendam
18. Langebaan
19. Namaqualand
20. The Cederberg

THE SOUTHERN CAPE AND CAPE INTERIOR
21. The Garden Route
22. Matjiesfontein
23. Oudtshoorn
24. The Valley of Desolation
25. Graaff-Reinet
26. The Augrabies Falls
27. Kimberley

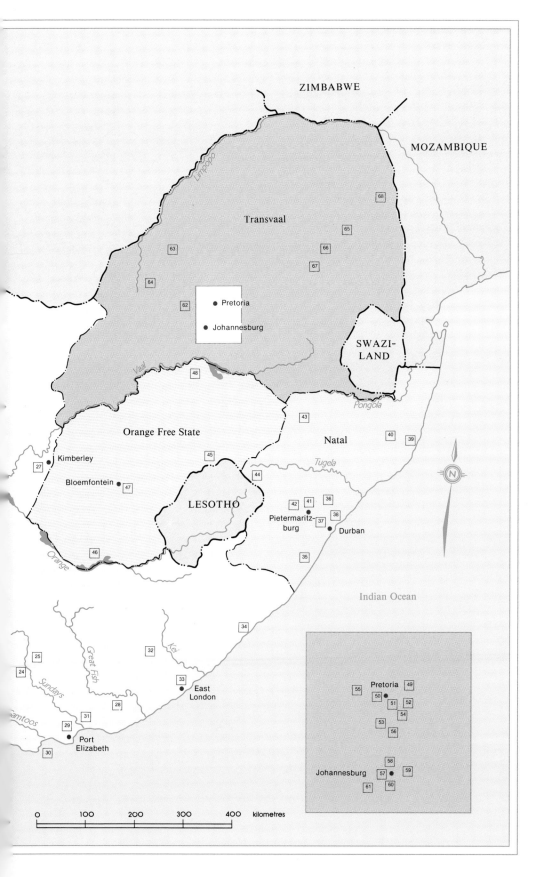

THE EASTERN CAPE AND WILD COAST

28. Grahamstown
29. Port Elizabeth
30. St Francis Bay
31. The Addo Elephant Park
32. Hogsback
33. East London
34. The Wild Coast

NATAL

35. The South Coast
36. The Valley of a Thousand Hills
37. Durban City
38. The Golden Mile
39. The St Lucia Complex
40. The Umfolozi Game Reserve
41. Pietermaritzburg
42. The Howick Falls
43. Rorke's Drift
44. The Drakensberg

THE ORANGE FREE STATE

45. The Golden Gate
46. The Hendrik Verwoerd Dam
47. Bloemfontein
48. Sasolburg

TRANSVAAL CITIES

49. The Union Buildings
50. Church Square
51. Pretoria Central
52. Pretoria Museums
53. The Voortrekker Monument
54. The University of South Africa
55. The National Zoological Gardens
56. Doornkloof
57. Johannesburg
58. Imperial Architecture
59. Ellis Park
60. The Mines
61. Soweto

THE NORTHERN AND EASTERN TRANSVAAL

62. The Magaliesberg
63. Ndebele Village
64. Sun City
65. The Panorama Route
66. Pilgrim's Rest
67. Sudwala
68. The Kruger National Park

INDEX